Effective Serious Games Development

This book showcases the entire lifecycle of a serious games project and guides the reader through different phases step by step. It follows a narrative approach, telling the story of a young game developer in a fictitious near-future setting who overcomes the challenges of a typical development process. The narrative is enriched by 15 short contributions from multinational experts on relevant topics for the development process of serious games.

This book describes a holistic approach to serious games development and follows a project from its very beginning to its end. It covers planning, creation, implementation and evaluation of a serious game. It does not cover technical details on how to write code or graphics for video games but rather focuses on the conceptualization of serious games and coordination between different roles and team members.

This book will be of great interest to beginners who want to use serious games to solve their problems. It will appeal to students of game development and also project managers who want to gain a better overview of the process as a whole and learn about tools and frameworks they can apply in their own context right away.

Philipp Busch is a game producer, designer, author and international keynote speaker. He teaches game-based approaches and agile methods at a variety of institutions and universities and learned his craft from cross-cultural teams all around the world. His company, Mind Games GmbH, supports the development of serious games for international institutions such as the UN, EU, FES, GIZ as well as the private sector and implements them in challenging global contexts. In his projects, he applies transparent, honest impact measurement and follows an ethical and sustainable development approach.

Effective Serious Games Development

A Step-by-Step Guide for Beginners

Philipp Busch

CRC Press
Taylor & Francis Group
Boca Raton London New York

CRC Press is an imprint of the
Taylor & Francis Group, an **informa** business

Designed cover image: Rebekka Schoenefuss

First edition published 2025
by CRC Press
2385 NW Executive Center Drive, Suite 320, Boca Raton FL 33431

and by CRC Press
4 Park Square, Milton Park, Abingdon, Oxon, OX14 4RN

CRC Press is an imprint of Taylor & Francis Group, LLC

ISBN: 978-1-032-61014-6 (hbk)
ISBN: 978-1-032-61013-9 (pbk)
ISBN: 978-1-003-46153-1 (ebk)
ISBN: 978-1-003-60947-6 (eBook+)

DOI: 10.1201/9781003461531

Typeset in Minion
by SPi Technologies India Pvt Ltd (Straive)

Contents

The Crackling Campfire...

Welcome! My name is Philipp, please take a seat next to me at the crackling campfire. Make yourself comfortable, get a drink and enjoy the salty breeze from the sea while I will tell you a story. You honour me with your time, so please allow me to introduce myself.

Welcome to the campfire!

I love playing games since I can barely walk. Of course, the games I played started simple. Still, I was quickly hooked, and the first time when

I immersed into a world of imagination in roll playing or boardgames, I was about 4 years old. This is also the time when I started creating my own games and stories, back than not much more than a lame copy of games I played before with my older siblings.

While growing up, the passion for playing and making games never stopped, and with my friends playing and inventing games became a central part of my life. I was already working in development aid when I explored the full potential of using games for more than just entertainment. I was fascinated by the idea of a scientific approach to combine serious and complex topics to create enjoyable, interactive experiences. That's when I decided to write my PhD on the use of games for global good, and for the past 10 years, I worked on projects all around the world in private sector and development aid, trying to address social and environmental problems through the use of one of the most interactive, socially connecting and natural artefacts of all cultures.

A game has the potential to support the formation of complex experiences in the players mind, no matter if we are targeting kids or adults who forgot how to play a long time ago. There is not a single culture on this planet that is not playing games. We can make use of this beautiful fact and use games as adaptable vehicles with the aim to contribute to global good. We can create unforgettable experiences and disseminate subject matter in a meaningful way. I worked on traditional enterprise-related topics like technology trainings, customer loyalty programmes or onboarding processes and also on topics such as peace support, sexual exploitation and abuse, reforestation, energy efficiency or human rights in fragile contexts, just to name a few. A game has the potential to convey any topic.

After reading this book, you will have a clear overview of the development process of serious games. It is meant to address not only beginners who start working in the games industry, but also for anybody interested in using serious games for their own purposes, for instance in companies or institutions. It is my interpretation of the learnings I made working with teams all around the globe. Consider the structure of this process as one of many possibilities. Every step can serve as a module that you can adapt, replace, erase or reshuffle. It serves as a starting point for reflection, for you and your team. You can start with it as it is, and step by step, you can tailor the modules you like to your needs and develop your own unique approach from them. Only then will the book unleash its full potential.

I wrote it being on a long travel developing serious games and learning from teams and cultures in 16 countries all around the world. Many learnings from this journey influenced the narrative of this book, and also enriched its learning content. The book was developed very similar to a serious game. A modern development process is a co-creative process making use of collective intelligence. I feel incredibly honoured and thankful to present you contributions by no less than 15 amazing guest authors from all around the world, who are much more experienced and smarter than myself and still were willing to share their wisdom with me, and now, with you. I invited veterans from the gaming industry and also experts from other relevant fields to form a heterogeneous mix of expertise and cultural background. You will find contributions from Australia, Brazil, Canada, Germany, Ghana, Italy, Jordan, Kenya, Mexico and the USA that are woven into the narrative of this book, still explicitly marked.

Storytelling is an essential part of this book. Next to hopefully make the reading more enjoyable, the story itself is filled with implicit learning and hints and underlines the social aspects of the development process. Allow me to invite you to a mind game to the future. I will show you my vision of what could happen, if humanity makes full use of the sheer endless potential of serious games. So let us begin.

STEP 0

Define Serious Games

Caspa loved the Academia Artis Ludi. It was a place of autonomous learning, individual mastery and intercultural exchange. The purpose of this school was offering free digital education for every person, regardless of age or background. Since the council of the wise declared free access to education for all, the university fees were obsolete. A huge boost for inclusive education, it became one of the most important pillars of the declaration of global rights after the crisis of 2040. In particular, educational and career opportunities for women were one of the main reasons why the earth's population found a natural balance and a sustainable life on earth was possible. There were still some major natural disasters, and the earth would take years to recover. But humanity managed to survive.

Caspa's parents didn't. They took him to his junior year at the academy. He still remembered when he turned around, seeing the tears of joy on his mother's face, for passing the test for the in-person boarding school programme. He still remembered seeing his father smiling at him, a rare occurrence. That day was the last time he saw them. Time has passed, and these wounds may never heal.

The young developer went excited through the wide corridor of the *homo ludens* building, attending a lecture of nobody less than the director himself, the famous Prof. Monty Goldhill. He saw many younger students entering the classroom, but he knew that way more would attend digitally. Just for fun Caspa activated the augmented mode of his glasses, and the new digital layer showed him hundreds of virtual avatars entering the room, who looked and moved identically as real persons who controlled

DOI: 10.1201/9781003461531-1

them in the analogue world. The university found out that realistic avatars would reduce the negative effects of digital anonymity; therefore, they had to match the real student behind. It was not the same as attending in real person, but it was good enough to participate in a lecture. The upcoming session was a famous one and basically every new student selected it: the definition of serious games. The *interactivum* was filled with physical and digital students, and the central stage was visible from every corner of the room. The conversations slowly became silent, as Prof. Monty Goldhill entered the room. He was a relatively short person with a big belly, bald head and an exceptionally long moustache, trenched in a long mentor's robe. Monty was very popular and admired by the students, but there were persistent rumours and bets about whether his moustache was real or fake.

The professor was followed by his personal assistance robot, the newest model of the Evolution 6 series. It was not bigger than a small drone, silently flying to the docking station of the plenary to project slides and material as a three-dimensional hologram, so every student was able to follow. Then the lecture began and as the professor started speaking, his voice and slides were translated simultaneously into hundreds of different languages and dialects, transmitted to all urban and most rural parts of the world.

Prof. Monty raised his pleasant voice: "I would like to share what I do understand under Serious Games and how it emerges and connects to similar fields. First of all, this is only my personal definition, and there are other definitions which are just as valid. Definitions are made to allow us structuring and categorizing the reality, and due to the limitless complexity of reality, the following definitions do not claim to meet all eventualities. From the perspective of a practitioner, they have proven to be usable. We require definitions to establish a clear communication in the development process, and many times I observed people who thought they would speak about the same matter, but their internal understanding was totally different, causing misunderstandings and failures. No matter which definition you chose, make sure that the people you communicate with are on the same page.

Look at this illustration. We could discuss each of these areas for hours; however, I want to give you a quick overview and simplified explanation. Please be aware that the term design is not meant as the creation of visual art, but as a conceptualization approach.

- Human centred-design (HCD): Mindset that puts the user into the centre of the design of products and services. Approaches such as design thinking are concrete frameworks within human centred-design.
- Behavioural design (BehaDe): Mindset with a specific focus to modify the behaviour and habits of the target group.
- Experience design (ExpeDe): Approach that designs for an intended experience of a human being. It aims to design the entire user journey of a user, while each experience is unique for each individual.
- User-experience design (UX): Optimizing the experience with one product or service like a website, but not designing the holistic user journey.
- Interaction design (InDe): Approach that aims for a high interaction between the user and product or service.
- Motivational design (MoDe): Approach to motivate user towards certain behaviour with a high focus on the psychology behind.
- Playful design (PlayDe): Designing experiences with defining allowed actions of the player with the intend of fun.
- Gamification: Design of playful experiences with a primary purpose other than pure fun.
- Game: Time-boxed experience where a player tries to overcome obstacles to achieve objectives to modify the end state of the game while following a set of rules.
- Serious game: A game developed for a primary purpose other than pure entertainment.

Let's have a closer look on gamification and serious games. The most famous definition of gamification is probably "The use of game elements and game-design techniques in non-game contexts"[1] (Werbach and Hunter 2012: 12). This definition is useful for giving people a first understanding of what gamification is, but as you dig deeper, you will notice some problems. For instance, it is really hard to define what a game-design element is, only because appearing in a game is not good enough to be called game-design element. Is a progress bar a game element? What about luck? What about a story? Even though these aspects are prominent in games, they don't belong to games only or were introduced in games first.

Also, too often gamification is understood as the simple use of extrinsic motivators like points, badges and leaderboards to trigger certain actions. Due to these problems, many practitioners who work in the field don't like the term gamification too much, but it found its way to public mainstream and stays quite persistent. Gamification is not about creating games; it is about learning from games to improve our interactive product design. We analyse successful games and try to understand the motivational structure that lies behind it. Then we extract and adapt this motivational DNA and embed it in solutions to solve real-world problems.

Let's discuss **games**. There are many definitions of what makes a game. In games, players can be humans, animals, and also artificial intelligence. Players can decide to play the game voluntarily or are forced to play the game. Think of a game like chess against artificial intelligence that you would like to play, a horse race or ancient gladiator games. These examples also show why I didn't include the voluntary participation in a game that Huizinga suggests in his book *Homo Ludens*[2]. Not only animals, but also humans are forced to play games, even though for them it doesn't feel like a game. You can also think of a boring math game that students are forced to play in class, for a less drastic example. Every game consists of obstacles or challenges that the player needs to overcome, either through knowledge, skill, luck or a combination. Depending on how the player overcomes the challenges, it can modify the end state of the game by reaching goals, and it might also be modified by other players or the system itself. The end state of the game can be binary and can also include many stages between absolute win and absolute lose. The set of rules forms a system with limitations and empowerments in which players are able to act. This means the player is not only restricted by the system, but can also be empowered to do things the player would normally not be able to do, for instance forcing another player to do a specific action. The limitations and empowerments are actually where we can spot a lot of fun of a game, but we will get to this later.

Within games I want to distinguish between **commercial games**, **hobby games** and **serious games**. Commercial games are developed for a primary purpose of earning money with the game directly. Usually, the player buys the game and receives a game experience in return. Hobby games are developed for a primary purpose of the developer's fun. The game developer can find fun in the development process itself or can experience fun while observing how other players interact with the game (Figure 0.1).

FIGURE 0.1 The pyramid of definitions.

In defining serious games, I put the focus on the initial person who is actually realizing the development of the game. What is their main intention? Entertaining a person or making money can still play an important role in the motivation mix of creating a serious game, and the initial and main reason is to achieve something else with a serious game.

In reality, a finished game has more than just one motivation, it is a **mixture** of many. Like a cocktail[3], the motivation behind developing a game consists of a variety of ingrediencies. Sometimes the main intention is clearly commercial. Sometimes the main intension is clearly serious, for instance if we want to train employees on cyber security by playing a serious game. But what about a serious games company that wants to create serious games for social good, however, still needs to pay its employees and therefore must sell their serious games? Perhaps we could speak here about serious commercial games. You see, the final product can be a mixture of different intentions.

We have a huge variety and own sub-categories within serious games. Learning games have the primary purpose to raise awareness, equip players with skills or change their habits and behaviour. Data mining games are collecting data from players through the use of a game, which can be used for instance to train algorithms, for user analysis, and also to recognize patterns in science. Marketing games try to raise awareness on a brand, increase customers loyalty and to make money indirectly.

Finally, you could actually **subsume serious games under my definition of gamification**. Serious games are also playful experiences designed for a primary purpose other than pure entertainment, and they just have some further characteristics to be called serious game. If a gamified system uses all these additional constraints, it actually is a serious game."

Caspa reflected on Monty's statements. Making definitions is the attempt of cutting the reality in smart pieces. We are trying to operate with these pieces, so we have to make them handy. Monty used in his definitions, the primary intention of the developer. From the **players' point of view**, these entire definitions played a less important role. The player might not be aware that they are playing a serious game or an entertainment game, because they have their own motivation to play that is totally different from the development process.

NOTES

1 Werbach, K., & Hunter, D. (2012). For The Win – How Game Thinking Can Revolutionize Your Business. Philadelphia (USA).
2 Huizinga, J. (1956). Homo Ludens. Hamburg.
3 Thanks Richard Durham for this metaphor.

STAGE A

Pre-Creation

CHAPTER 1

Phase 1

Initiation

Caspa attended the lesson for a specific reason. He was about to finish his studies at the academy and loved the idea of realizing games for global good, inspired by the serious games initiatives of recent years that have helped to make life on this planet worth living. Caspa had a vision. And 3 weeks ago, he decided to make it happen.

STEP 1.1 DEFINE A PROBLEM

There was a problem that Caspa wanted to solve. When he arrived at the academy, he not only felt helpless because of his terrible loss, but additionally was overwhelmed by the mass of information in the academy with no clear structure. It was just too much. There were many books on the specifics of game development, and for a beginner, it was very easy to get lost. Every team and game studio in the world seemed to follow their own approach. Graduated developers rarely had an overview about the entire process and were just specialized in their corresponding field of expertise, for instance coding. Furthermore, project managers or commissioners of private companies or international institutions that wanted to make use of serious games as a tool to solve a problem couldn't find an easy approach that allowed them to understand, follow or steer the process.

Caspa's vision was to give an easy-to-follow overview about serious games development. His mission was to create a step-by-step guide in the format of a modular serious game that could be adapted to the needs of any

DOI: 10.1201/9781003461531-3

team. Caspa's strategy was to give this serious game to the academy and to private companies so upcoming serious games practitioners could play and learn from the game. Before he could start with the development of his game, he had to get more information about the process for himself. How to develop and steer a serious game from cradle to grave? That would define the subject matter of his solution.

STEP 1.2 BOOTSTRAPPING

Caspa wanted to bring his idea to life and started to work on a first prototype of his game idea, so far only consisting of pieces of paper and a notebook with roughly defined rules. Caspa started his project bootstrapping, initiating the game process himself without external resources. Caspa knew many games that were not linked to bigger publishers or game studios and still celebrated big successes by bootstrapping. He also heard of the term venture prototyping, related to venture capital, in which individuals and teams are investing their own money in the prototype to get the project initiated.

A big advantage of bootstrapping or venture prototyping is the freedom that Caspa faced. He was able to fully unleash his creativity without external limitations. He invested his spare time in his prototype, staying up late night in a state of total concentration and flow. He also paid his peer Yuki from the art department some drinks in exchange for initial concept art. After endless hours, his first prototype was done. Caspa was convinced that he created something very special, a serious game that was so innovative that it might have the power to revolutionize learning. He was excited playing the prototype with his friends, but then reality hit him hard. The game didn't really work the way he had imagined, and the feedback from his friends was not only polite but also devastating. Nobody wanted to play the game again, instead one of his friends said: "Ok, now let's play a real game!"

That was the first lesson Caspa learned. Your initial game is not as good as you believe. Nonetheless, Caspa was resilient. He improved his prototype and changed his approach entirely, and after playing the game with his friends a few more times, it became better. Caspa knew he was about to do something meaningful, and he really saw an added value in his idea. Bootstrapping could be continued for years and be successful, but Caspa wanted to change his approach. He needed some external funding right now. Caspa picked up his notebook and went through his high concept note.

STEP 1.3 CREATE A HIGH CONCEPT NOTE

There were many different possibilities to structure a high concept note (HCN), also depending on the sector and what you wanted to achieve with it. Caspa created the HCN to request initial funding. It was of high importance that he knew about the background and the current situation of the recipient of his HCN, in this case: Prof. Monty. Caspa found out that the professor was not happy with the introduction class of serious game development for new students, so Caspa sensed an opportunity to solve a problem. He decided on the following structure.

HIGH CONCEPT NOTE STRUCTURE

- Cover – An eye-catching illustration, the name of the game and the authors.
- Problem statement – Problem combined with a personal story that the reader can relate to. Ideally the problem is backed up by relatable data to show the scale of the problem.
- Solution – The solution in the shape of a concrete yet initial game approach and how the subject matter is incorporated.
- Vision statement – The one sentence that summarizes the game.
- Game in action – The situation, place and context in which the target group interacts with the game, giving a tangible idea how the implementation of the game could look like.
- Market and target group – Ideally with demographics and a first number of potential users.
- Existing solutions and USP – Competition and why the proposed game is of added value, ideally illustrating the unique selling proposition (USP).
- Team – The development team and supporting stakeholders.
- Timeline – Time including different stages, phases and milestones.
- Financials – Including development costs, price building and potential profits.
- Requests – Call to action or concrete request to the recipient, for instance required funding.
- Contact information – Website, social media and one concrete contact person.
- Summary – Most relevant information clearly compiled on one highly visual page.

FIGURE 1.1 The commissioner Professor Monty.

Sometimes the HCN was also called pitch document, game vision document or vision statement document, since the slide with the vision statement was the core of presenting the new solution.

Caspa named his game *Crunch Time* and formulated the following vision statement: "Crunch Time is a fast-paced competitive 1vs1 serious game in the shape of an analogue card game in which 2 players try to build the best serious game possible within certain limitations, playing process, tool and team cards to improve the quality of the game while throwing threat cards onto the opponents serious game development."

Caspa knew about the influential power of aesthetics, so he made sure to invest enough time for formatting and including initial illustrations, the concept art. He kept the text as short as possible, sticking to one message per slide, going for a dark background with high contrast and following the famous sentence of "A picture tells more than thousand words."

After the interactive part of Prof. Monty's session, Caspa nervously adjusted his student's toga, then approached his potential commissioner (Figure 1.1).

STEP 1.4 ONBOARD THE COMMISSIONER

In serious games, the commissioner is the person or institution that has a problem and provides the development team with a budget to solve it. This could be individuals, private companies, institutions of development aid, investors, funding bodies, participants in a crowd-funding campaign or game publishers. The commissioner is the stakeholder providing the necessary funds, but in most cases is not equal to the target group, who is playing the game once released. The commissioner is usually limited in time and needs to manage many projects at the same time. Sometimes, the game is in a different shape of what the commissioner expected at the beginning, and this might have its reasons. To overcome the challenges ahead as a unity, it is important to always maintain a transparent, trustful and honest communication between the commissioner and the development team.

Caspa knew that whoever provided him with money, this entity had certain expectations that he had to fulfil. If Caspa would seek for several independent stakeholders providing him with budget, he would face a situation of cross-financing, in which he would need to satisfy the needs of different commissioners, and sometimes they even have mutually contradictory objectives which require clarification from the very beginning. He decided to go for a single-commissioner approach for the start.

"Ah Caspa, it is you, great to see you. One of my best students in the academy, if I may say so. I heard you didn't go to the prom last week but asked for allowance to leave the academy to spend the night on your boat instead. How much time has passed since the terrible event? I am sorry, I didn't mean to offend you, I am just concerned. Please my dear, join me in the elevator and let me know how I can help you."

Caspa swallowed the rolling wave of grief: "5 years, Sir."

The professor invited him to the elevator. "Again, I am very sorry. But I can see that this is not the reason for your visit. How can I help?"

Caspa took a deep breath. He knew that he had not many chances reaching Prof. Monty, he would be on a research trip very soon. This short elevator pitch was his biggest chance. Luckily, Caspa practised it several times. You had to clearly communicate a solution to a problem or create a new need that was not there before. You had to be careful not to overtax your elevator pitch audience. Caspa called it the innovation meter. 100% innovation would be something that was never there before, something humans could not even think of yet. Unfortunately, even if these innovations would be of great added value for the world, sometimes the market is not ready for it yet and therefore the innovation fails in its implementation. 1% innovation would be a small improvement to a problem or creating a tiny new need. Caspa estimated that for his purpose in this elevator pitch, 20% innovation would be a good option, solving an existing problem with a well-known format, but combining aspects in a new way leading to a superior design. Casper finished his pitch on time, and the door of the elevator opened after 30 seconds.

"Very interesting. I have a couple of minutes to spare, please follow me to my office."

They crossed different halls and finally arrived at the office. Caspa was disciplined enough to not overdo the pitch, while Prof. Monty opened the big wooden door with fine carvings of game artefacts of dice and ancient consoles. Caspa was in the office just once and took a seat in front of the huge desk, which was crowded by a chaotic mix of papers, books and IT equipment. After showing the professor his high concept note, Monty pondered in silence before continuing.

"You are almost done with your studies. Your time at the academy is over for now and thanks to your excellent performances in the past, I want to offer you something that I have never offered before. I will bring you in contact with the Mind Games Initiative to gain a first-hand understanding of the process."

Caspa was stunned. The Mind Games Initiative consisted of living legends. Many years ago, they worked together with experts from all over the world on the crisis simulation of 2040, which was one of the most important events in the past centuries. This simulation was the first game accessible by almost all humans, which created a persuasive experience how the world would be like in 20 years, if exploiting capitalism, national corruption and the destruction of the planet wouldn't be stopped. Too often in history, human beings needed to experience a catastrophe first before change was happening. But the simulation empowered by artificial intelligence was so immersive that it felt real. Humans were able to simulate their own extinction, and this milestone combined with a terrifying increasement of horrible natural disasters caused the biggest change process of governmental structures and economic systems in history. Independent international institutions with the support of the artificial intelligence NESGA developed an all-changing action plan to secure the survival of human beings. Due to massive awareness raising campaigns, this substantial change process luckily went hand in hand with a global cultural change, which was called the "awakening."

Prof. Monty was also part of the working group of the simulation, but while the Mind Games Initiative went to the operative part to implement the NESGA plan, Prof. Monty went to the academy to train upcoming generations of developers.

"It is your mission to arrange the logistics. As I know the Mind Games Initiative, they are somewhere spread across the globe. For your project, I will be the commissioner and providing you with initial funding. As you know I am quite busy, but you will have to inform me and get my approval for all major decisions. Good luck on your journey, Caspa."

CHAPTER 2

Phase 2

Framing

CASPA WAS ONE OF the students living in the academy area. He had his digital notebook in his hand, lying on a swing in his cozy room. Plants were all around, and his window was wide open giving him a stunning view over the green campus. One silent drone was flying close by, fertilizing the moss layer of the outer wall which caused a nesting bird to chase it away. A problem the developers still had to fix. But there was another problem that Caspa faced. He was reading through the initial requirements that Prof. Monty sent him.

STEP 2.1 ELABORATE ON INITIAL REQUIREMENTS

These requirements were not really detailed or elaborated, actually it was quite vague. Caspa pondered whether Prof. Monty did this on purpose to demonstrate how a commissioner usually formulates the initial requirements, or if he was really too busy to think it through. Caspa was biting his fingernails, and he hadn't noticed that one was bleeding slightly. He read through the requirements again.

DOI: 10.1201/9781003461531-4

DEAR MR. CASPA,

Thank you for your pitch. I will grant you an initial 15,000 USD to work on the game treatment and for your travel expenses. These are my requirements:

1. Create a serious game on serious games development with a playtime of maximum 60 minutes.
2. The learning content should include all project steps from project initiation to project closing.
3. At least 5.000 students have to play it before the end of the project.
4. The format of the game should be an analogue boardgame.

I already informed the Mind Games Initiative about your enquiry. The overall timeframe of the entire project is 18 months. After receiving your game treatment, we can discuss a potential continuation as well as additional budget for marketing. I added a contract for the current project stage.

Kind regards,
Prof. Monty Goldhill

STEP 2.2 SIGN THE CONTRACTS

Caspa knew that many contracts include certain exit points, allowing the commissioner and the contractor to back off from the project. This gives both parties a certain security, so there is not one huge budget to be spend at the beginning of the project, but progressing step by step in case the project progression finds mutual acceptance. The modular contract approach from Prof. Monty looked like this:

Contract Period	**I**	**II**	**III**	**IV**
Phase	Conceptualization	Construction	Pilot Phase	Upscaling Phase
Potential Exit Point after...	... submitting the game treatment	... submitting the pilot version	... implementing the pilot version, improving game and submitting the master version	... implementing the master version and submitting the final report
Budget	20%	60%	75%	100%

The first contract period consisted of creating a game treatment, including all necessary steps to get there. If the treatment was convincing, Prof. Monty could approve the next phase, the construction of the actual pilot version of the game. If the game was good enough, the professor would spend additional money for the first implementation, improving the game to the master version. If the pilot was a success, he would approve the last phase, implementing the game in more contexts and receiving a final report on the entire project. This breakdown just served for an initial overview and probably the budget percentages would be redefined along the process.

The high concept note is often attached as an Appendix. However, it is important to mark in the contract that this document just serves a starting point. The shape and format of the game will most probably change after going through a proper analysis and iterative design phase. Caspa knew that this was a potential point of conflict. From the perspective of the commissioner, they want to know as much as possible for what they are signing the contract for. What genre and setting will the game have? Will it imply a multiplayer mode? In the high concept note, there is already a sketched solution, a potential shape that our game might have at the end of the process. In one of the lectures, there was an example of a very immersive 3D virtual reality game that was promised, teaching kids how to behave responsibly in traffic. Following the process of analysis and iterative design, the team found out by speaking with the kids and understanding their context in detail that a 2D casual game playable on low-end smartphones would actually lead to way better project outcomes. In the contract, both parties signed for this 3D virtual reality game, and the commissioner was not flexible enough to accept the new shape, causing the project to not reach its full potential while burning a lot of money.

There were two ways how to handle this problem. One option was to work with modular contracts as Prof. Monty did. The other option is to go with one big contract including all phases. Then, the best way was to not fix the final shape of the solution but to achieve the goals with the most suitable shape. The parties could agree going for a serious game and perhaps specify an initial shape of the game, but the commissioner needs to be aware that the initial approach could change entirely throughout the process.

It was time to get started. It was time for his expert interviews. Caspa was about to visit a legend of serious game production: The first of the Initiative.

Caspa sat in a public compartment of the underground train to the green city. He was nervous. As a preparation for the upcoming meeting, he watched one of his favourite Mind Games Blinks of the past. He clicked on the play button, and a 3D hologram of the legendary Troy Dunniway appeared. Caspa switched to the augmented mode of his glasses to not disturb the other passengers. The video began.

GUEST BLINK TROY DUNNIWAY, USA – THE ART OF GAME PRODUCTION

Troy Dunniway has been designing and producing games for over 30 years and worked on over 100 AAA PC/console games at Microsoft, EA, UBISOFT, Disney and many other studios. He has run teams from 3 to 3,000 across the world and his games have sold over 4 billion copies in over 70 countries. He is a consummate jack-of-all-trades polymath who is part designer, artist, engineer, producer and leader. He is also the author of several books on game design and development and teaches game design at CG Spectrum.

As a video game producer, there are a million different things you may need to be responsible for. You need to be a jack of all trades who understands most aspects of how a game goes from ideation to completion and maybe even how to operate it live. The video game producer is ultimately responsible for keeping the entire project on track from inception to launch. To be successful, a game producer must have a firm grasp on game design, development (processes, pipelines), scheduling, marketing, budgeting, outsourcing, legal, QA & focus testing, communication and team management. More senior-level producers will need to have a more strategic level view of the project and be able to create and manage a long-term plan, while others working with them might handle more day-to-day details and management.

Game production requires overseeing multiple teams spanning many disciplines like art, design, engineering, music, testing, etc. The producer is the cohesive force that ensures all of these groups are working in sync towards the same goals. They must be an excellent manager of people and resources – coordinating schedules, resolving conflicts, providing feedback and removing blockers. The producer sets the cultural tone, tempo and processes for the entire project.

Probably the biggest challenge a producer faces is communication. Being a producer requires beyond exceptional soft skills which are often underestimated. Producers need to drive meetings, emails, slacks, team communication, teammate to teammate communication, executive micromanagement, manage up and down to the executives and team, shield the team from unclear messaging, manage external influencers like publishers, manage outsource teams and more. The producer is the communication "glue and the grease," which keeps a team together and keeps the gears running. Some days you are a glorified babysitter, referee, therapist and cat herder. But underestimating how the communication breakdowns on teams is the biggest cause of failure, which is probably the biggest mistake a producer makes. You can't assume everyone knows what they need to know, you need to double check, verify, enable, empower and sometimes force it on a team.

As part of the problem related to communication is how the creative vision of the game is created and held by the game director or creative director. A producer is often more responsible for the feasibility of the games design and production… That is, can it be done, and also be done on time and on budget with the team and technology. A producer helps keep the creative vision in check, helps to make sure it is not too big, helps to validate it with users and with data (through focus testing), helps evangelize the project to executives, while also helping other leads by acting as a buffer between them and outside influencers and stakeholders to help them manage the wide assortment of various feedback elements and demands being asked of the games creatives, while also helping them manage all of the changes and stuff up to executives, licensors and publishers. This can help the creatives focus on being creative, while the production team helps keep them focused and doing what they do best as much as they can. Some executive producers (like myself) are also design savvy and can help as a sounding board for creatives as well or be more involved in the creative side of a project to help creatives who are overly busy or maybe lack some skills in some areas as games are incredibly complex to create. This is usually a dotted line relationship between equals who help to balance each other to try and make the best game they can.

As a producer, the biggest job typically is managing the schedule of a project. One of the biggest challenges in the industry however is that current production methodologies in game development are extremely misunderstood and most teams struggle with being waterfall, agile, hybrid or some mix of many things. Most producers don't actually understand the concepts well, and most scheduling tools are not great either, which often leads to problems. However, the biggest issues often come back to communication, and lack of prosper decisions and specifications. Many teams, and especially game designers, use agile methodology as an excuse to "find the fun" and therefore not document or actually do proper upfront designs with enough details that producers cannot properly schedule things. Or in contrast, some teams over design upfront, leading to the creation of long documents which get out of date and are unusable. This inherent conflict leads to probably 90% of the scheduling issues in games and is the biggest issue with keeping teams on time and on budget. This also gets amplified with the "shiny ball syndrome" which designers and executives are often guilty of chasing the latest trends or fads and cannot focus, causing teams to constantly get sidetracked or spending time on things that aren't actually needed. So producers need to work closely with design teams to try and manage this incredible complex problem. Knowing what to design and when and knowing how to make decisions and keep teams focused is a critical producer skill they must master.

One of the biggest mistakes producers also make, which relates to both communication and scheduling, is not doing strategic planning. Many teams don't understand Agile methodologies properly and only tend to plan 1-2 sprints ahead (so 2-4 weeks into the future), which leads to a tremendous amount of failure as they get too focused on the micro or tactical implementation of things and don't track, understand and plan for what the final game needs to be competitive and viable as a long-term product. This is also a symptom of improper planning and designing and can lead to massive failures. Some teams take a bottom-up approach in production, and they just implement one feature after another, without understanding their context and how they fit into the big picture. A more top-down approach can lead to much better strategic planning, and help teams understand what they still need to do and by when. This can also help producers properly plan when they know the rough scope and scale of the finished game which needs to exist to be competitive versus just building the game until you are "done" (usually when you run out of budget or executive patience).

There are infinite sources of potential risk in game development – creative differences, engineering blockers, talent leaving, overspending, a shift in market conditions, you name it. The producer must have a sixth sense for identifying risks early and creating mitigation plans. Producers need to be resilient problem-solvers who expect the unexpected and are always mapping out multiple contingency options. They need to constantly evaluate any and all known and unknown risks and constantly build in proper contingencies which can help the team adapt to when (not if) small or massive problems or changes occur from internal issues to external factors out of the control of the team. Producers need to see where the risks are and plan for the worst.

Conclusion

So, as a producer, remember to build your soft skills, learn as much as you can about each team, each person, each process and everything you can related to the games production, people and processes. With so many crucial responsibilities, it's easy to see why veteran video game producers are in such high demand. To successfully bring a game from concept to shipping product requires someone with remarkable organizational skills, creativity, technical knowledge, business savvy, and most of all, unflappable leadership abilities. It's an incredible challenge and also an immensely rewarding career for those with the drive to deliver premium interactive entertainment experiences to millions of fans worldwide.

STEP 2.3 MEET THE GAME PRODUCER

The train arrived in the green city a few hours ago, Caspa sat in a waiting room.

"You may enter now."

The well-dressed robutler opened the magnificent double doors in perfect symmetry. A gust of fresh air blew towards Caspa, a pleasant scent of carnations and roses caressed his nose. He walked carefully into the office of the living legend. The interior was perfectly structured and consisted of functional yet elegant furniture, just as much as necessary, but nothing that didn't serve a purpose or distract the eye. The room was crowned by a huge desk formed by transparent plastic. The material was pressed into a solid form using the latest upcycling procedure. Caspa was initially surprised by the contrast, a celebrity like Mrs. Prombu could surely afford a desk made of pure gold. But then he understood. Caspa exhaled deeply. A glass door to a sweeping balcony stood wide open, the light of the early sun reflected in the clear structures of the architecture.

"I am outside. Please come, the overview is fantastic!"

Caspa walked respectfully through the balcony door as the outlook let him speechless. They were on the highest floor of the Sus Tower, probably the most impressive architecture on earth. Each floor had its own style, but at the same time was part of an overarching, all-encompassing masterpiece that reflected the biological network of the planet. The rising sun bathed the fascinating scenery of the green metropolis in an auspicious light.

"Isn't it wonderful?" A tall, dark-skinned woman turned to Caspa. She was wearing an elegant, modern business attire combined with selected artefacts from her African origin. Caspa gulped when he saw how tall she was. Her graceful features underlined by dark eyes indicated an impressive intelligence, her charisma and presence were overwhelming (Figure 2.1).

"Look what we created when we finally got things right and took our true place in world."

Huge towers, overgrown with moss and flowers, stretched upwards like green termite mounds. The transportation tunnels were barely visible through the dense canopy of vegetation, and here and there Caspa spotted people on tree platforms chatting or having a coffee in semi-nature.

"I always wanted to see the green city, thank you so much for accepting this interview."

"It is a pleasure. As Monty sent me the message about your inquiry, I became curious and checked your high concept note. It is promising."

FIGURE 2.1 The game producer Prombu.

Caspa sighed. "I didn't know he would send it to you. I thought we would just have an expert interview on serious games production? I watched the video of Troy Dunniway on game production as a preparation, are you familiar with it?"

"I am. Serious games production is all about communication with internal and external stakeholders and managing the project with a specific focus on timelines and budgets. In smaller serious games projects, the producer is also responsible for all legal aspects like contracting, licences or handling intellectual properties. Furthermore, the producer manages the finances, paying bills or writing invoices. When we founded the Mind Games Initiative, I was responsible for the initial contact with our commissioners. They either approached us or in some cases, we approached them with a pitch deck.

As a serious games company, we have business interest in realizing many projects; it is important to note that serious games are just one possibility to reach the target, and most of the times they are only one piece of the entire solution mosaic (Figure 2.2).

Is a serious game really the best choice? Sometimes, a short video is enough, you don't need an interactive experience just for the sake of having it. Don't get me wrong, I am obviously a huge fan of solving problems through serious games, but a first big mistake is going for a serious game when there would be a more efficient option.

FIGURE 2.2 Serious Games as a key piece in the mosaic of global problem-solving.

Prombu asked Caspa to deliver his elevator pitch. After a few clarifying questions from her, Prombu smiled: "Congratulations Caspa, you convinced me. I believe in your project, and for now, I believe a serious game is the best tool to solve the problem. I will support you with the production of your serious game, in case you accept my offer. I hereby offer you my mentorship."

Caspa was stunned. He stuttered: "O-of course, it would be an honour! I didn't expect that. I thought I would just interview you and... Well, I thought that would be it."

"It sounds like a relevant project for us all. Let us continue with size and complexity."

STEP 2.4 DETERMINE THE SERIOUS GAME SIZE

From the perspective of a game producer, time, team and budget are the most important factors that determine the quality of a serious game.

The estimated size and complexity of a project will allow us to get a better idea of our limitations. Let's use an old Serious Games Project Size Scheme (SGPSS) as orientation.

Serious Games Project Size Scheme (Version 2024)				
Project Size	**Budget (in USD)**	**Additional Marketing Budget (in USD)**	**Project Duration**	**Team Members**
Tiny	<25.000	<5.000	<3 months	1–3
Small	25.000–150.000	5.000–50.000	<12 months	3–10
Medium	150.001–500.000	50.001–200.000	<18 months	5–15
Large	500.001–2.000.000	200.001–700.000	<36 months	10–20
Mega	>2.000.000	>700.000	>36 months	20+

Obviously, this scheme is just a very rough classification tool, a rule of thumb. It doesn't take into consideration inflation or future AI developments, varies between sectors and is just valid for the year 2024. Also, the marketing budget varies highly depending on the chosen game format and context. Nonetheless, it can be useful for beginners to get an idea of what kind of budget, time and team is required to create a serious game.

Prof. Monty gave you an initial amount of 15,000 USD to create the game treatment, with potential follow-up contracts leading up to 250,000 USD in total, plus additional marketing budget, making this a medium project.

I will inform the rest of the team. Having the right team on board is perhaps the most crucial aspect of the entire process. Let's have lunch and then I want you to meet another key role in each serious games project.

STEP 2.5 MEET THE CREATIVE DIRECTOR

Before he knew what happened, Caspa had lunch with Prombu and now was sitting in a workshop room that seemed to be designed to unleash creativity. There were digital boards, sticky notes and pens all around, while music and illumination automatically adapted to the mood and the task of the guests. The window wall offered a stunning view over the green city. The door opened, and Caspa's eyes widened when he saw who entered. It was Derren Gandwe, the creative director of the Mind Games Initiative. Derren was a handsome man, his long black hair was tied into a bun, a well-groomed three-day beard underlined his angular facial features. He wore a *critca*, a rope that formed a whole from numerous patches. But most remarkably, Caspa could feel a charismatic fire when Derren entered the room. Caspa immediately felt a certain zest for action, he wanted to perform as good as he could.

Prombu smiled at Derren: "May I introduce you to my husband Derren, the creative director. Producer and creative director should be in the meetings and planning sessions together as soon as possible, and it is of great added value that we both come along so well." Prombu winked (Figure 2.3).

FIGURE 2.3 The game director Derren.

Derren had a clear and deep voice, that was both pleasant and determined: "You must be Caspa, very pleased to meet you. I heard you came a long way from the academy. What brings you to us?"
After Caspa introduced himself and his inquiry, he had to ask the question: "Mister Derren, what is it that you actually do as a creative director in serious games?"

"As a creative director or game director, I am responsible for overlooking the entire creative aspects of the game. Both producer and director should know the entire project by heart, but while the producer is mainly focusing on the realization of the project and setting limitations, the creative director tries to maximize the quality of the product within these limitations. I should be involved in the main communications with the commissioner as well, but my main focus is on the internal team. The creative director is a senior expert and should have experiences in game design, programming and art in order to support the team members and unleash their full potential. As a team, we overcome obstacles and I try to ensure an efficient balance of self-determined work and central decisions. Within game design, programming and art, there are thousands of big and small decisions to be done during the process. The creative director holds the strings together so the entire game is goal-oriented and follows a clear vision. Depending on the size of the project, I am also responsible for the design of impact measurement systems, so creating systems that allow to proof that the game is actually fulfilling its targets.

Depending on the size and complexity of the game, I coordinate all people who are in creative team, namely the designers, programmers and artists and jump in if necessary. Furthermore, I communicate with the subject matter expert and the game designer on a frequent basis, so the serious aspect of the game is embedded into the core of the game. In smaller teams, I can take over every role in the creative team, most often I take the role of a game designer. Finally, I am responsible for an ethical and inclusive game approach."

Caspa hesitated: "Could you elaborate what you mean by that?"

"There is a terrific Mind Games Blink on it, I think it fits well here. Robot, please play the video by the genius Melinda Jacobs."

GUEST BLINK MELINDA JACOBS, GERMANY: SERIOUS GAMES AND ETHICS

Melinda Jacobs is a product expert, gamification specialist and N7 paragon with over 12 years of experience. She's a geeky nerd who found a way to combine her love of games and her fascination with people's behaviour into an award-winning expertise. She's worked with companies of all sizes from small start-ups to large, multinational enterprises. As Mindstone's Co-CEO, she's on a mission to help people upskill in the skills that matter most for humanity, starting with AI.

As designers, it's our duty to continually question, evaluate and refine our practices with ethical practices at the forefront. Understanding how your users might be affected by your design, both positively and negatively, is essential in order for you to take responsibility for the possible impact. Thinking about ethical implications helps ensure that your experience is respectful, fair and enjoyable for users.

Let's quickly dive deeper into the essence of three key ethical considerations: accountability, transparency and autonomy. We'll look at why they are important and how you can start to effectively implement it in your work.

Accountability in Serious Games

As well stated by the University of Helsinki, "Accountability is an acknowledgment of responsibility for actions, decisions, and products" [https://ethics-of-ai.mooc.fi/chapter-3/2-what-is-accountability]. At its core, accountability in serious games is about accepting responsibility for the behaviour and impact of your system. It's not just about creating an engaging experience; it's about acknowledging the role that your experience (may) play in the lives of the people who use or experience it.

In order to be accountable, you need to have a deep understanding of the potential impact or consequences of the design decisions you make and how they (might) influence user behaviour. Understanding your role in shaping user experience is key, and an ability to have introspection is vital, in general, for ethical design practices.

Accountability doesn't just protect users, it builds trust and credibility for your system/experience. When users know that a platform is designed with their well-being in mind, they are more likely to engage deeply and meaningfully with what you've created. Trustworthy systems open the possibility to create a loyal user base and significantly influence the overall sustainable success of the product.

Key Questions: Checking for Accountability

To ensure you are accountable, you should constantly reflect on and address several critical questions throughout your design process:

Are you willing to be accountable for the decisions you make and the events that unfold in your experiences?

Have you anticipated misuse and considered how your system could be exploited by bad actors, thereby exposing users to risk?

Are you willing to be transparent and honest with users about the purpose and functioning of the game elements and system?

Do you understand your own values and intentions in the design process?

Are you willing to acknowledge mistakes and if necessary apologize and make a correction?

Autonomy in Serious Games

According to The Ethics Centre, "Autonomy is the capacity to form beliefs and desires that are authentic and in our best interests, and then act on them" [https://ethics.org.au/ethics-explainer-autonomy/]. Autonomy in game/gamification design is a design that allows users to make independent decisions without undue influence. This allows users to act in their best interest versus merely following a (manipulative) design.

Key Questions: Checking for Autonomy

To check on how much autonomy your design allows for, try and reflect on and address these questions throughout your design process:

Is opt-in the default setting in your experience versus opt-out? Opt-in requires users to actively consent to participate in or use a service or aspect of the product, whereas opt-out automatically enrols users, requiring them to take action if they do not wish to participate.

Do you ask for user consent before taking (hidden) actions?

Have you made some tasks more difficult to complete to discourage or limit certain actions? If so, why?

Are users provided with enough information to make informed decisions? Are they aware of what's going on behind the scenes that could be influencing (or making) their decisions?

How much influence are you applying on the decision-making process? Are users acting out of understanding or pressure?

Are you facilitating, guiding or controlling user action within you experience?

Transparency in Serious Games

Once again, let's go to the University of Helsinki on transparency. Transparency is "about how much it is possible to understand about a system's inner workings 'in theory'." [https://ethics-of-ai.mooc.fi/chapter-4/2-what-is-transparency] In short, in design, transparency is an open, honest and straightforward communication that makes information accessible to users. It's about ensuring that the inner workings of your (game) system are clear and understandable.

Key Questions: Checking for Transparency

What data are you collecting and why? Is this clear to the user?

What behaviours are you encouraging and how clear is it what impacts they have as well as the motivation behind having users complete this?

Is there easily accessible content, tutorials or explanations about your product/experience that users can access to understand how it works?

Are the results of your system clear and accessible?

Are your motives for building the system transparent?

Thinking about Accessibility

Accessibility in games and gamification is pivotal in ensuring autonomy, transparency and accountability for all users, regardless of their physical, cognitive or sensory abilities.

Accountability in accessibility means that designers and developers must commit to ongoing assessment and improvement of their systems, actively seeking feedback from users with disabilities and incorporating it to address barriers.

Autonomy is enhanced when systems are designed inclusively, allowing users with diverse needs to navigate and interact with the game independently. This includes implementing features such as customizable controls, screen readers and adaptable difficulty levels, which empower users to have their experience personalized and modified according to their abilities and preferences.

Transparency is vital in this context, as users need clear information on the accessibility features available and how to utilize them effectively. Obvious if they're not aware this is an option, they cannot use it. This can be achieved through detailed documentation, tutorials and user-friendly interfaces that communicate these options straightforwardly.

Impact of AI on Ethics

AI will, and is, impact games and gamification design by making possible enhanced personalization and immersion, and also introduce critical challenges to consider related to autonomy, transparency and accountability.

From an accountability perspective, AI-driven systems require oversight to ensure ethical standards are maintained. Designers and developers must be accountable for the decisions embedded within AI algorithms, which includes anticipating potential misuse and addressing biases that could lead to unfair or harmful outcomes. This involves implementing robust ethical audits (e.g., the check-ins like we explored earlier) and continuously monitoring the system's impact on users over time.

Additionally, accountability, as mentioned before, also means being prepared to rectify issues transparently and promptly when they arise. This means maintaining an open dialogue with users about any changes or updates made to the system, especially as AI can be "black box" in its operations.

AI can customize experiences to individual users by analysing their behaviour and preferences, leading to highly engaging and motivating environments. However, this level of personalization can undermine your user's autonomy by subtly guiding their actions and decisions without their explicit awareness. It can also lead to situations where users are unaware of what they are opting into and can be manipulated without realizing it.

When AI systems are not transparent, users may not understand how their data is being used or why certain elements are presented to them, which can lead to a lack of informed consent and control. This opacity can erode trust, as users may feel manipulated by the system rather than empowered by it.

Therefore, again, ensuring transparency in AI-enhanced games or gamification involves clearly communicating how data is collected, processed and utilized, providing users with the ability to opt-in or opt-out of personalized features.

Conclusion

As designers, it's imperative to continually question, evaluate and refine our practices with an iterative mindset that keeps ethical considerations at the front. Understanding the potential positive and negative impacts of your designs on users is essential for taking responsibility and ensuring respectful, fair and enjoyable user experiences. Experiences that stick to these principles of accountability, transparency and autonomy are the ones that create genuine behaviour change and learning that leads to lasting impact rather than short-term, misunderstood engagement.

Derren summarized: "Ethics is a cross-cutting topic that need to be incorporated in the entire process, therefore the creative director is a good choice to be responsible for this important matter. All right, my love, what comes next?"

STEP 2.6 CREATE AN IMPACT INTENTION MATRIX

Prombu took a pen and stood up: "We formulated our initial vision, did a successful pitch and received initial requirements of the commissioner. Now it is time to translate these requirements into smart goals, targets, KPIs and declarations. A goal is an overarching objective that I want to achieve with the game. A target is a quantifiable measure how a goal can be achieved, and thus a goal can have a variety of linked targets. KPIs are specific trackable values within a target, and hence a target can consist of a variety of linked KPIs. A declaration defines the terms within our goals and targets, to make sure the team speaks about the same things.

Let's check the first requirement of Prof. Monty.

Requirement 1: Create a serious game on serious games development with a playtime of maximum 60 minutes.

Goal (G) and Priority	Linked Targets (T)	Key Performance Indicators (KPI)
G1: Create an analogue serious boardgame on serious games development (High priority)	T1: Create a learning experience on serious games within 1 year. T2: Select the right format of the serious game. T3: Design a playtime of maximum 60 minutes. T4: Empower players to pass the Mind Games Level 1 assignment after completing the game. T5: 80% of the players rated the game with "Very Good" in the post questionnaire.	KPI1: Development time KPI2: Playtime KPI3: Mind Games assignment level KPI4: Percentage of players KPI5: Player rating

Declarations

- Player: Person from the target group who is playing or has played the serious game.
- Target group: Enrolled student in the university "Academia Artis Ludi."
- Playtime: The net duration of the playtime experience without set up or pack up of the game.
- Mind Games Assignment Level 1: Existing knowledge check on serious games development.
- Passing Mind Games Assignment Level 1: Answer at least 80 out of 100 questions correctly.

As you can see, we added targets that are not in the initial requirements. Very often, just following the commissioner's requirements would not lead to real impact. We need to set ourselves additional targets and benchmarks in order to create meaningful interventions. Like a previously closed flower, the petals unfold as the goals, targets, KPIs and declarations are clarified and we can explore what is under the surface. This approach has another positive implication. If we have worked out the impact definition before the creation stage, the game concept and desired actions of the players can be designed to our goals in a much more targeted manner.

Our game designer can make the learning experience integrative, rather than sequentially adding learning content on top of the game experience afterwards.

In the impact definition process, be sure to keep track of the big picture as you enter the rabbit hole. Each declaration can lead to further declarations. Don't lose sight of the overarching goals and maintain your common sense."

After Prombu, Derren and Caspa polished the impact intention of Caspa's game *Crunch Time*, they conducted a mandatory digital meeting with the commissioner, agreeing and adjusting the refinements. Caspa was proud. The project just became much more goal-oriented.

STEP 2.7 SELECT YOUR TEAM

Caspa watched the cleaning robots taking a break, taking a recharging sun bath on the balcony where he first met Prombu, who wore a colourful dress that day. Each pattern seemed to play and interact with the other, with no clear dominance or hierarchy of a single colour.

Prombu took the word: "Recruiting the right team for the project often is the responsibility of the producer. Depending on the complexity, size and context, you will select your team accordingly. Different projects require different roles and responsibilities. Also, the amount of team members depends on the complexity and budget of the project. I will show you the team roles and responsibilities of most of my serious game projects.

1. Game producer – Manages timeline, finances, contracts, team, legal aspects and represents main communication point to the commissioner and further project-related stakeholder.
2. Creative director – Coordinates creative aspects and team to maximize game's quality. Maintains the creative vision and direct the work in a goal- or impact-oriented way. Responsible for an ethical and inclusive game approach and impact measurement systems.
3. Subject matter expert – Gives input on the subject matter or learning content of the serious game, supports in content integration and impact measurement.
4. Ex-Coms specialist – Manages the external communications or public relations to networks, markets and the target group by

analysing current trends while communicating audience requirements to the team.

5. Game designer – Conceptualizes the game, defines genre and setting, creates rules, levels and stories, embeds the subject matter into core game experience, etc.
6. Visual artist – Creates and animates all visual elements including sketches, concept art, final assets, visual effects, etc.
7. Sound engineer – Composes, selects and integrates soundtracks, sound effects, interactive audio. Potentially manages musicians as well as instrumental and voice recordings.
8. Programmer – Responsible for all technical aspects including the construction of code, integration of art and game design, set up of server structures, publishing the game on stores, etc.
9. QA officer – Responsible for focus testing, feedback and bug reporting as well as running internal and external testing rounds.
10. Localization expert – Translates the game into the local languages and checks subject matter or learning approach for cultural appropriateness for the different target groups.
11. Evaluation expert – Collects and evaluates the data that is produced within the entire serious games project.

"Thank you for this overview. Do you always need that many people working on a single serious game? Initially I thought I would do the entire thing just on my own..."

Prombu nodded and smiled: "This is just a selection of roles that nicely represent the different areas of serious games development. Please be aware that this is not equal to the amount of people working on the project. Depending on the complexity and budget of the project, you can have hundreds of people working on a single game, with way more specialised sub teams. We see these huge teams in the creation of so-called AAA-games, so games that have big budgets and expect big revenues. On the other side of the spectrum, it is also doable that you take all the roles mentioned and follow the entire process just by yourself. Many independent studios just work with teams consisting of 1-3 people, which can also lead to outstanding results. Smaller teams shouldn't get scared by this list. The people in the team can take over multiple roles in the process (Figure 2.4). For instance, the person in the role of the game director might also take

FIGURE 2.4 The gathering of the development team.

over the role of the game designer, the visual artist is also the sound engineer and the producer takes over the role of ex-coms.
It is also possible that you have several people of your team in the role of a game programmer, which is the case in most projects, which requires to define a lead programmer role. It depends on the requirements of the project and the variety of skills of your team members. Therefore, it is so important that you have an experienced producer who selects the right people and is able to allocate and adapt appropriate roles and responsibilities.

Make sure to sign contracts with your team members, transparently communicating the circumstances of the project. In our case, Prof. Monty went for a modular contract approach, incorporating potential exit points which might cause the project to stop early. It is always a good idea to get professional support by a lawyer for the team contracting, especially when you work in international contexts."

Prombu opened a window: "We received green light for the game treatment. In the case of our project, we can now officially sign contracts for the roles of the producer, game director, ex-coms specialist, subject matter expert and game designer. No worries, you will meet them one by one. For now, we will continue with the process map."

STEP 2.8 ADAPT YOUR PROCESS MAP

A process map or road map will help you and your team keep the overview of where you are in the process. We need a structured process to reduce the complexity of the reality, making progress operational and allowing for orientation. From my experience, every team choses their own approach, refining and improving their processes each time they go through it. Changing key roles in a team, working on new game genres in new contexts requires to adapt the process accordingly. What worked for this one project might not work for the other anymore. Nevertheless, we need a starting point. What I want to offer here concludes the best practices from the past 10 years working on serious games with teams all around the globe. This process is called the Mind Games Doctrine and is separated into stages, phases, steps and cross-cutting assignments (Figure 2.5).

As you can see, I separate the serious game development process into the stages pre-creation, creation, implementation and post-implementation. Pre-creation is everything you do in order to set up the project, doing the research and gaining as much relevant information as possible. Creation includes concepting, constructing and testing of the game as well as community building. Upon implementation, we run the game with our target group and upscale it. In post-implementation, we do a final evaluation, see what we can recycle from the game, close the project or hand it over. Each stage is populated by different steps, concrete actions that you can do in order to move on with the project. No worries, we go through all the steps at a time.

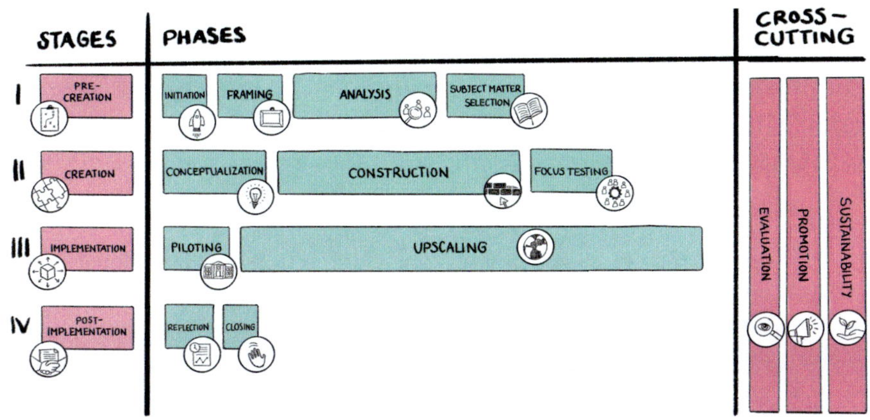

FIGURE 2.5 The Mind Games Doctrine.

The cross-cutting assignments are related to tasks that you should consider running throughout the entire process. Evaluation refers to the constant tracking of positive and negative impacts that you have on the world throughout the entire project, once you have a game constructed. Cross-cutting promotion goes hand in hand with community building and is something that I advise teams to do on a frequent basis, no matter in which phase they are. Finally, an ethical mindset reminds us to act responsibly on an environmental and social level in all stages of the process. I truly believe the importance of this way of thinking can't be stressed enough.

This model is designed in a modular way, so every team can select and adapt the stages, phases and steps to their needs. It also allows to reorder the modules in a way that best fits the project. For instance, you could already have very early implementations with real users in a workshop just using a very early prototype of your game, and in parallel improving it to a mature version of the game. Sometimes it is also necessary to go through a phase several times, running phases in parallel or reusing a step from a previous stage in the current one. As always, it is a tool that should serve the team, not the other way around.

STEP 2.9 AGREE ON YOUR DEFINITIONS

We face a big variety of definitions among different teams. For instance, I heard teams using "production" in many different ways, either meaning the entire process, the construction of the game or the creation of analogue material. It does not really matter which definition we use as long as all relevant stakeholders use the same. New teams need to do a semantic check and ideally having their own little wiki or agreeing to an external source that defines the necessary terms. I decided to go for these definitions in order to reduce the miscommunication between people from the gaming industry and traditional project managers or the commissioner in serious games projects.

- Serious Games Development – The entire process of game development, from the initial idea to the closing of the project, combining the work of all disciplines. The process of serious games development consists of stages, phases and steps.
- Stage, Phase and Step – A stage is a part of the entire development process that consists of relating phases. The end of a stage

marks a big milestone, nevertheless a team can jump back to a previous stage if required. A phase is an ongoing or timeboxed period which is characterized by a predominant work and consists of different steps. Different phases can overlap. A step can be an activity, event, the use of a tool, method, etc. to drive the project forward.

- Serious Games Production – The type of work that is done by a serious games producer. It includes team composition, scheduling, budgeting, coordinating and communicating with external and internal stakeholders to realize the game.
- Serious Games Creation – A process stage which includes game design, game construction and testing. Along the game creation process, several prototypes and game versions will be created.
- Serious Games Design – The work that is done by a serious games designer. It includes the creation of the game rules and concept of gameplay, the narrative, events and story, the decision and adaptation of the genre and setting, the creation of game loops, the ongoing process of balancing of game values, etc.
- Serious Game Conceptualization – A phase in the process in which most of the game design work is done. It consists of ideation, selection, prototyping, testing and the setup of the game design document.
- Serious Games Construction – This phase covers the software engineering, game programming, art creation including visuals, sounds, animation, incorporating the game design and merging it all into a working analogue or interactive game. This is the phase where concepts evolve into working software in digital products or constructing material for analogue products.
- Serious Games Manufacturing – A step in which tangible material will be created, either the entire analogue game itself or supporting material for a digital game.
- Serious Games Implementation – A stage of the process in which the game is rolled out, including publication in stores, distribution, delivery, piloting or soft launching, upscaling, live-ops as well as running analogue workshops to use the serious game with the target group.

Derren continued the process: "I just created an internal wiki and added the definitions. Let's set up the monitoring environment."

STEP 2.10 SET UP THE MONITORING ENVIRONMENT

The projections of the robutler illuminated the room, while Prombu explained the tables:

> "The monitoring environment will help us to keep track of all necessary project indicators and enables us to react to problems, to overcome obstacles but also to celebrate progress. Depending on the complexity of the project, you need an equivalent management system to handle this complexity. Similar to an octopus, the system must be flexible enough to adapt to the movements of the environment and be able to react to changes over time. Neither does it makes sense to work without monitoring systems at all, nor shooting at sparrows with cannons. The selected tools need to serve the project, not the other way around. There are professional tools to track this overall progress, but you can also create your own dashboard for smaller projects, consisting of the tools that are of added value. In the following, I will introduce you to the tools that might be useful for our project."

STEP 2.11 SET UP A HIGH-LEVEL SCHEDULE

Next to the process map, you should use high-level schedules to keep track of the time. These are classical tools in project management and basically visualize the timeline and milestones of different project stages, phases or steps. Next to keeping track of the overall deadline and the milestone deadlines, they visualize phases that take place in parallel.

Of course, you can also go more into detail and add milestones or project steps. You can also select different time units for it, going for quarters, months or even weeks. Plan the buffer time depending on the complexity and uncertainties. For instance, add some buffer if your team has never worked on the chosen game genre before or if you are highly dependent on external inputs that are not under your direct control.

STEP 2.12 SET UP A BUDGETING TOOL

Constraints of time and budget are the biggest enemies of game producers. From my experience, the question is not "if" but "when" we will run out of budget. We need to allocate the budget between the

EXAMPLE OF A HIGH-LEVEL SCHEDULE.

Stage	Phase	Time																					
Pre-Creation	Initiation	■																					
	Framing		■																				
	Analysis		■	■				■	■														
	Content selection			■	■	■	■																
Creation	Conceptualization			■	■	■	■	■	■	■	■			■									
	Construction				■	■	■	■	■	■	■	■	■	■	■	■	■	■					
	Focus Testing						■	■	■														
Implementation	Piloting									■													
	Upscaling										■	■	■	■	■	■	■	■					
Post-Implementation	Reflection		■	■	■	■	■	■	■	■	■	■	■	■	■	■	■	■	■				
	Closing																						■
Buffer																				■	■	■	

salaries of the team, equipment, licences and server costs, programmes and assets, promotion and marketing activities, travel expenses, workshops, testing rounds, production of analogue material, and also costs for implementation, events and reporting. Furthermore, projects should add a budget line for compensations for negative impacts, keeping in mind that our activities might cause negative environmental or social implications. Similar to the timeline, we also should have buffer for the budget. The more complex, uncertain or new a project is, the bigger should be the buffer. As a rule of thumb, I usually plan with a buffer of 20-30% of the overall budget. It never happened that I haven't spent this buffer at the end of the project in a useful way, so don't think that you will have to squander it at the end. If you have a project team that is working for many years together on very similar projects, than you might just need a buffer of 5% or none. However, I highly recommend working within harder limitations, afterwards you can always add more nice features to the game. But if you ran out of budget and you don't have a product to implement or budget for the implementation itself, you are in trouble.

Use a tool that fits your requirements. A simple table might be sufficient for small projects, while a professional tool allows you to keep all the different budget flows together, for instance revenues through analogue and digital purchases, in-app advertising, licences, etc.

Expense Item	**Amount**	**Costs/Rate (USD)**	**Total (USD)**
Producer	5	1.000	5.000
Game director	4	1.000	4.000
Ex-Coms	4	800	3.200
Subject matter expert	1	800	800
Game designer	4	800	3.200
Concept artist	1	800	800
Travel expenses	2	500	1.000
Sustainability compensation costs	1	2.000	2.000
Total			**20.000**

This would be a very simple example for our first contract period. Please be aware that daily rates for experts heavily vary depending on the country and expertise.

GUEST BLINK MICHAELL QUINN PATTON PHD, USA: SERIOUS DEVELOPMENTAL EVALUATION FOR SERIOUS GAMES

Michael Quinn Patton has five decades of experience as a professional programme evaluator. He is the author of ten major evaluation books including Developmental Evaluation (Guilford Press). He is former president of the American Evaluation Association.

To make evaluation meaningful and useful for serious games, I would suggest that 12 traditional rules of the evaluation game itself need to be transformed. That transformation takes the form of what I have called Developmental Evaluation[1] (Patton, 2011), which is a process for evaluators to support innovation and adaptation throughout a creative process. What I am proposing here would build on that approach, so to distinguish its application for serious games I will refer to it here as Serious Developmental Evaluation (SDE). What follows is a way of integrating evaluation into gamification that constitutes serious developmental evaluation[2] (SDE) for serious games.

1. Evaluation, as traditionally approached, places the evaluator outside and external to what is being evaluated. This is to ensure evaluation's independence and objectivity. But what it really does is increase cluelessness. In contrast, an SDE evaluator is involved with the serious game creator throughout the gamification process. This has the advantage of letting the evaluator learn and understand the internal logic of the game and therefore be able to bring the logic of evaluation to play in a more meaningful way. That doesn't make the evaluator biased. That makes the SDE evaluator relevant and knowledgeable.
2. Evaluation traditionally occurs at the end of a process when the game is uploaded and disseminated. Occurring at the end, the traditional evaluator has the responsibility of making an overall judgement about the merit, worth and significance of what has taken place and the game's impacts. In contrast, the value of SDE is increased by making it an ongoing part of the gaming process providing feedback and insights in each step of the game's development, not just at the end.
3. Traditionally, when evaluation is external and at the end of a process, it is thought of and approached as an add-on, something extra added to the serious game process. In contrast, SDE is embedded in the process and makes evaluative thinking a way of doing business, part of the creative process, not an add-on, but integral to gamification. When you are determining desired impacts of the

game, you are engaged in evaluative thinking. When you are then designing for impact, you are engaged in evaluative thinking. When you are conceptualizing how the game will achieve the desired impacts, you are articulating a theory of change, which is intrinsically based on evaluative thinking. When you are mapping how serious gaming contributes to other aspects of a training programme or intervention, how gaming fits into the whole, you are engaged in evaluative thinking. Serious evaluative thinking as manifest in SDE can undergird all aspects of serious gaming.

4. Traditional evaluation emphasizes rendering an overall judgement of merit and worth called "summative evaluation": Does the game work? Does it attain the desired outcomes? These are simplistic questions. In contrast, SDE supports ongoing learning and adaptation. SDE provides feedback and insights for ongoing development, innovation and adaptation. This includes continuing evaluation once the game is uploaded and being used, meaning that the app includes the capacity to generate data about use and provides mechanisms for users to provide feedback about their experiences and impact pathways that emerge in their use of the game. That feedback may inform subsequent versions of the game as well as provide generic learning to apply to future gaming design. Instead of simply asking "Does it work?" we ask "What works in what ways for which people with what outcomes in what contexts?" That is a fundamental SDE question.
5. Traditional evaluation makes the evaluator the expert judge of effectiveness. In contrast, SDE is a process where the evaluator facilitates evaluative reflections by game participants. SDE is participatory evaluation so that participants in the game deepen their experience of the game by reflecting on and evaluating that experience.
6. Traditional evaluation treats rigor as a function of methods. But methods are just methods. Rigor resides not in the methods but how they are used and that use depends on serious evaluative thinking. That thinking is engendered through serious questioning. Participants are asked: What was playing the game like for you? What do you take away from the experience? What aspects of the game, if any, were difficult or confusing in some way? What aspects of the game were especially engaging? What will you do with what you learned from playing the game? These are examples of SDE participatory evaluation questions.
7. Traditional evaluation tends to value qualitative data as a way of getting precise results. SDE for gaming uses both quantitative and qualitative data. Qualitative data are answers to the

kind of questions listed above (point # 6) while quantitative data involves creating rating and reaction scales for participants to provide feedback about elements of the game. A mixed methods approach provides general findings from quantitative data combined with the in-depth insights that come from open-ended narrative qualitative data.

8. Traditional evaluation follows the psychometric measurement principle that evaluation should not have an impact on the thing evaluated. Measurement instruments are designed to minimize what is called "participant reactivity." In contrast, SDE for serious games can design and implement evaluation to deepen the experience of participants so that the reflective process built into the game enhances the experience and learning from participating in the serious game. Building reflection into the game makes evaluation part of the intervention both in real time through immediate reflection and longer term as reflective questions may prompt thinking about ways to build on the gaming experience, thereby increasing the game's impact. This is especially true at the interface between the experience of being in the game and the potential application of learning from the game that can be applied in the real world. Building into the game a "magic-in-game circle" and real-world interface makes serious reflective evaluation useful for stimulating action in the real world. The validity of this approach to evaluation resides in its transparency and intentionality in that the SDE is designed to be part of the intervention. Some will view that as bias. I view SDE as increasing utility and impact.
9. Traditional evaluation would tend to treat evaluation of the serious game as an end in itself, focusing only on the game experience and outcomes. But because serious games often are part of a larger process of learning and engagement so a SDE would take a comprehensive approach so that the evaluation of the game is designed as part of a larger system evaluation that includes examining the other learning activities and engagement opportunities of which the serious game is but one part. SDE is holistic and comprehensive in nature, which means understanding the serious game as part of a larger complex dynamic system and placing the evaluation process and findings in that larger context when appropriate.
10. SDE is culturally responsive evaluation. Traditional evaluation tends to be generic, standardized and generalizable. But because serious games are used in different cultural settings, the evaluation

process must be adapted to those cultural and contextual variations meaning the evaluation and the game are both culturally adapted and responsive. One aspect of the SDE, then, is ensuring that the game is culturally responsive, meaningful and appropriate – and treating those characteristics as evaluation criteria.

11. Traditional evaluation tends to focus on individual outcomes in education. But serious games are meant to have an impact not just on individuals but on groups, organizations, communities, and even, potentially, national and international institutions. SDE, taking a systems approach, can design evaluation to assess impacts on these different units of analysis – and should do so. One emergent possibility is using AI to assess participants' reflective feedback while playing the game to give them real-time comparative information about what others are experiencing. This can be done with groups of people who know each other, but it can also be used in a broad-based dissemination of the game where players get more general information about how their experience is similar to or different from other players, with AI constantly updating the data.
12. Traditional evaluation aspires to assess the attribution of an intervention to a predetermined outcome. In gaming this means showing a direct causal link from the short-term experience of the game to a longer-term impact on people's thinking and behaviour. That kind of thinking is closed-system linear causality thinking. When dealing with complex systems, where gamification is part of other forms of engagement and educational interventions, we move from attribution analysis to contribution analysis. This means examining how a serious game interacts with other aspects of the intervention to contribute to observed impacts. Contribution analysis is narrative (story) based, not unlike story-based gaming. The evidence for contribution comes from follow-up, the opportunity for which is ideally built into the app.

Conclusion

Serious gaming and its impacts can be enhanced through serious developmental evaluation (SDE).

STEP 2.13 SET UP THE PROJECT IMPACT SYSTEM

Next to keeping track of budget, time and product progress, we should set up the project impact system to ensure a goal-oriented procedure. Evaluation is an integral part of the entire project, not only an activity that should be done by outsiders at the end of the process. The producer is responsible to set up the general impact system of the entire project and keep track of it, while the creative director is responsible for the impact measurement systems in the game. Both should be aware of all management tools at all times.

Derren agreed and turned to the robutler: "There is a famous Mind Games Blink by the famous evaluation legend Michael Quinn Patton. Please play the video."

The blinds went dark and the recording was played.

> As Michael Quinn Patton in the video was explaining, evaluation is something that should be seen as a cross-cutting topic. The positive and negative implications of the project start directly with the very first activities, so don't wait with the measurement until you have a final product. For instance, interviewing the target group on the topic of climate change will probably have a positive impact on them, even if the project is cancelled afterwards. On the other hand, your flight to the interview location implicates negative effects, taking into consideration the carbon footprint. Furthermore, there might be unexpected impact that you initially did not intend to cause with your project, but still might be relevant to track to receive a more holistic perspective. Let me elaborate on this.

STEP 2.14 TRACK DIFFERENT TYPES OF DATA

What types of impact can we measure? Accurate data collection is a complex matter, especially given the overwhelming complexity of reality. In order to proceed in a more structured way, I differentiate between direct quantitative and qualitative data as well as indirect quantitative and qualitative data (Figure 2.6).

Direct data is data that we gain directly from our project activities and is collected in a planned manner according to our initial impact intention with goals, targets and KPIs. Indirect data is data whose collection was not planned in advance, but is nevertheless relevant for the project evaluation. Quantitative data is numerical data, while qualitative data requires interpretation. These four categories can be presented in a matrix.

I will start with **direct quantitative data**. Let's assume we would have a digital version of the game in a digital store. Depending on where we publish the app, we can already draw a lot of direct quantitative data from

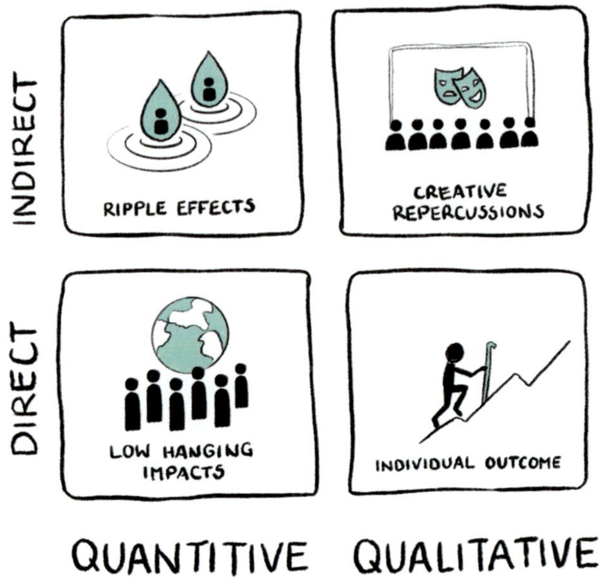

FIGURE 2.6 Data types for impact measurement.

the admin area of the platform. However, we can also integrate our own tracking systems to the game to provide us with additional data. There are existing tools to track the activities of your user, so you don't need to build everything from scratch. When integrating such a tool, attention must be paid to the applicable data protection guidelines, as some systems store the data on external servers that do not necessarily comply with our guidelines. Unfortunately, many projects determine their success just by observing direct quantitative data, for instance the number of downloads. Viewed in isolation, however, this data says very little about the true impact. We need to dig deeper and combine it with the other data types, understanding how people interact with the app and what ripple effects come with this interaction.

I continue with **indirect, quantitative data**. Our project could have effects that were not intended by us, but are still relevant. For example, a vivid community in another part of the world could be established as a result of our game, running own analogue tournaments with hundreds of new players. Consider fan wikis with thousands of entries describing different aspects and characters of the game. We can track number and types of community content on fan sites, designing their own levels, stories and characters, unofficially expanding the game world. Our game could be used by networks and schools that we didn't have in mind, depending on how we define the rights of further use. Influencers could test the game and inform thousands of streamers about it on their channel. Indirect, quantitative data by definition is unpredictable, but if we become aware of the data, it can be relevant to approach a more realistic and holistic impact report. A small stone can set several stones rolling.

Quantitative data provides a solid foundation for our impact measurement, and should be completed by qualitative data.

Measuring **direct qualitative data** is realized in a planned manner, but interpretation is required. Classic examples are interviews that we conduct with our target audience after playing the serious game. Individual impact and personal stories about whether and how a small aspect of our target group's life has changed after playing the game is valuable information, for instance how people now perceive refugees after playing a serious game on involuntary migration. In addition to interviews, comments and written evaluations of our game would be relevant, for example, discussions in forums that we were setting up as part of our community management. We can also interpret and evaluate creative contributions from our target group, for instance if we initiate a content competition on art for peaceful coexistence. These impacts can be assessed not only at the individual level but Úlso for institutions, systems, and beyond.

Indirect qualitative data is data that requires interpretation and its creation was not intended by us. It can be extremely valuable, but is hard to collect. For instance, creative content published on fan pages that requires interpretation from us as evaluators. Similarly, a network of former players could be formed as a consequence of the implementation workshops of our game, who keep up a regular exchange on reforestation in the region. After playing a serious game on nutrition, a group could positively change other aspects as a result of the initial change of the key habit of nutrition. The group might not only have adjusted their diet, but also exercise regularly, established a healthy sleep rhythm and inspired friends and family with their behaviour. A negative example would be that people feel addicted to our game, which could imply negative effects in other aspects of their life.

That said, make sure to incorporate **positive and negative impacts** to obtain a realistic picture of the intervention. Many projects don't track or eliminate negative impacts which is certainly not a transparent and honest evaluation practice. There are exceptions, for instance handling the data produced by trolls and bots that actively publish deconstructive feedback, usually with a background thought and would obviously bias the impact evaluation. This feedback should be collected by the evaluator as well, but can be excluded from the impact report by explaining the exclusion criteria.

STEP 2.15 SET UP SHARED WORKBOARDS AND ADDITIONAL MONITORING SYSTEMS

We will speak about a product backlog later in detail in the construction phase, but already now you should set up a backlog, workboard or shared to-do list to keep track of all necessary tasks and their progress in the upcoming phases. A very simple one could look like this.

ID	Work Package	Priority	Responsible	Tasks	Status
1	Do target group analysis	High	Caspa	• Set up questionnaire • Conduct 30 interviews • Create persona	Pending
2	Explore additional implementation options	Low	Caspa	• Do online research • Speak to Prombu	Pending

Obviously, you can go in more detail and add more columns to describe the work packages. You also see that the second work package is totally blurry and not well defined, which is also fine and good enough for now. Get an overview about all tasks and keep those that are better defined and more pressing on top, while keeping the ones that come along the way blurrier at the bottom until it is their time to get revised.

Next to the presented systems, you could add additional monitoring systems to your monitoring environment. Especially working in cross-cultural teams, I like to add a team satisfaction system, in which on a bi-weekly or monthly basis the team should anonymously answer three questions regarding their satisfaction, giving them the possibility to express potential frustrations or share constructive feedback with the team. Another handy tool is a community progress system, keeping track of your followers or brand awareness. One tool that you should always use is the stakeholder map, and let's speak about this in detail."

STEP 2.16 CREATE A STAKEHOLDER MAP

In order to carry out a project, you need an overview of the stakeholders. Next to being in frequent contact with the target group and your internal team, you will communicate and establish cooperation with external stakeholders, increase your professional network, collaborate with commissioners, additional subject matter experts, freelancers, teams from private companies, governmental and non-governmental institutions, etc.

Every project offers the possibility of making new contacts, and these contacts might not only be relevant for the current project, but even will help you to initiate or join strategic alliances, professional networks in which the stakeholder support each other to achieve shared goals. Even if your game might fail horribly, you might establish important connections that will help you in future projects. Of course, low performances can also affect connections negatively.

The stakeholder map I use is a four-field matrix which visualizes interest, potential influence and attitude of an external or internal stakeholder towards the project. The **project interest** identifies whether and to what extent the stakeholder wants to have an impact on the project. The **potential influence** describes the extent of the stakeholder's impact on the project in case the stakeholder becomes active. The **attitude** classifies how positive or negative the stakeholder's attitude towards the project is an can be visualized by using a colour code, red for negative attitude, yellow for a neutral, and green for a positive attitude (Figure 2.7).

"I think I understand. The matrix is not only providing me with an overview about the stakeholders, but also suggests recommendations for actions. An external stakeholder with high interest, high potential influence and a negative attitude must be ideally turned into a collaboration partner. A stakeholder with high interest, low influence and positive attitude could be informed about the project's progress. We could start negotiations with a low-interest, high-influence, neutral-attitude stakeholder to turn it into high interest and positive attitude. Finally, a low-interest, low-influence stakeholder with negative attitude should be observed without having a concrete requirement for action at this moment."

"Correct. It's a practitioner's tool, sometimes the action tags like "negotiate" or "collaborate" don't make sense in certain situations, so use your common sense or adapt it to your needs. The producer keeps the map up to date, so it doesn't lose its functionality."

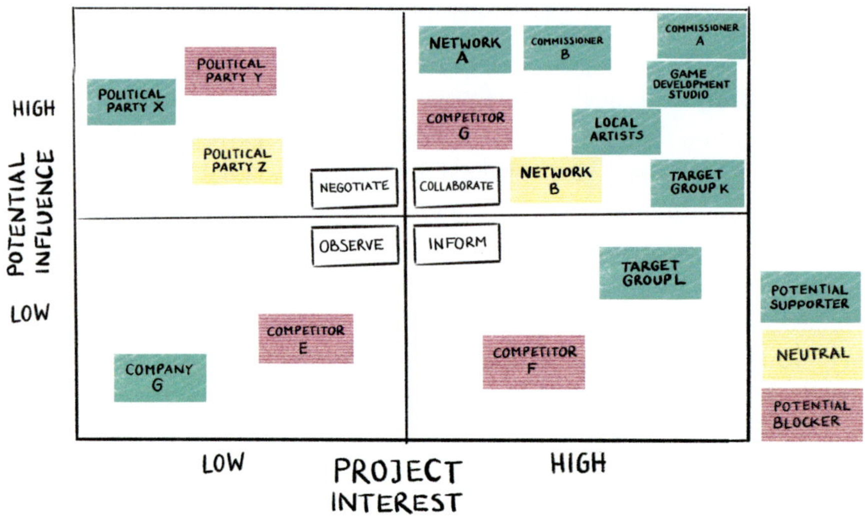

FIGURE 2.7 A typical stakeholder map.

Prombu continued: “The stakeholder map usually builds the bridge between the phases framing and analysis. This means, you have to find Anaka. It is time for a travel.”

NOTES

1 Patton, M.Q. (2011). Developmental evaluation: Applying complexity concepts to enhance innovation and use. Guilford Press.
2 Patton, M.Q. (2023). The niche and purpose of developmental evaluation. YouTube video: https://youtu.be/X9CplOFsHZ8.

CHAPTER 3

Phase 3

Analysis

WITH EVERY STEP, CASPA's boots sank a little into the sand. He laboriously struggled along the edge of the dune. The young developer would never have expected his journey to take him to such a hostile environment, but there was no way he would ever give up. He saw his father's face in his mind's eye.

According to the oasis inhabitants, Anaka had left for the desert and had been living with a local tribe for several weeks. How anyone could survive in such heat was beyond Caspa's imagination. The air was hot and dry, and despite his best physical efforts, Caspa felt like he was barely sweating. Any moisture was instantly absorbed by the dry desert air, leaving only a white crust of salt on his clothes to testify to his physical exertions. His guide was clad in airy clothing. He seemed to be less bothered by the intense sunlight, as the dark clothing protected him better from ultraviolet radiation, which was another thing Caspa learned from the local. He heard the big man's real voice before his in-ear headset translator kicked in.

"We are almost there. The Kirlinos[1] settlement is behind the next dune. Drink more water."

Caspa gratefully followed his guide's advice and took a deep swig from his canteen. His assisting robot, a state-of-the-art homunculus with advanced spatial intelligence, flew a few metres above them, a precious gift from Prombu and Derren. Caspa was not good in giving names, so he called it Evali. While the sun was burning the energy out of Caspa, the little robot was doing exactly the opposite thanks to its solar panels.

DOI: 10.1201/9781003461531-5

Caspa realized that Evali was processing data waiting in its storage for a moment like this at full power inception. The latest update of the energy efficiency protocol seemed to be working well. Slowly, Caspa struggled up the huge dune until he sank exhausted to his knees at the crest. A valley spread out in front of them, where dozens of tents had been erected. Camels rested in the shade of large awnings, while an outdated, four-legged transport robot dug a hole with a clunky shovel module. Men and women in colourful robes supervised its work and assisted the robot with shovels, while children ran laughing through the rows of tents.

Caspa entered the temporary camp, for the Kirlinos were nomads living in symbiosis with their environment. Exhausted, he sat down on a rock and took the last sip from his canteen. While his guide was in search of Anaka, Caspa watched the work on an irrigation channel that tapped into the groundwater. Then he saw a female student sitting in the shadow, wearing a very old VR-goggle (Figure 3.1). Caspa was stunned as he recognized her. He knew her as Tangesh994, a fellow peer from the academy! Of course, he was just in contact with her virtual avatar until now, but Caspa was surprised that even in the far desert, people were accessing the academy.

FIGURE 3.1 Accessibility problems of the target group.

Tangesh seemed upset, cursing in local language. Caspa's in-ear device activated, recognizing what Caspa was currently focusing. He heard Tangesh's voice speaking to her mother: "Damn, no connection again. Prof. Lawin's simulation is simply eating up too much bandwidth for streaming. And my processor is too old to take over the calculation." Caspa was surprised, he thought that since years the global connection was optimized and simply perfect. Tangesh stood up, throwing the old VR-goggle in the sand and went into a tent. In the moment Caspa wanted to follow to say hello, his guide came back. He pointed to the construction site.

"You friend is over there in the manhole."

STEP 3.1 MEET THE EX-COMS SPECIALIST

Confused, Caspa forgot his exhaustion, thanked his counterpart and climbed down into the pit. The men and women at work interrupted their work and eyed the newcomer curiously. Caspa raised his hands uncertainly.

"I am looking for a person called Anaka. They are supposed to be here. Anaka. Are you here?"

A nondescript person emerged from a group of working people. They wore the same robes and had a similar stature. The person was tanned by the sun and had bright blue eyes that seemed to miss nothing. Delicate yet calloused hands pulled back a hood and revealed colourful, iridescent hair tied back in a bun. Anaka had no obvious gender, and Caspa knew that they were polygender and thus identified to all genders (Figure 3.2).

"It is nice to meet you. Caspa, I suppose? My name is Anaka. I have some work to do before it gets even hotter. Just lend a hand and we are done soon."

Caspa was puzzled but agreed, picked up a shovel and couldn't remember the last time he had exerted himself so physically. It got hotter with every hour. At first, the work organization felt confusing and chaotic. But blending into the group, he recognized a sophisticated system in which the nomads supported each other with the heavy work, resulting in surprisingly quick progress. Anaka supported them, but also carefully observed every detail, took notes and pictures with a watch camera without disturbing. Caspa was surprised at how well Anaka had already integrated into the community. He communicated verbally and non-verbally without pushing himself to the fore. They were like a chameleon, blending into the work, absorbing and copying the socio-cultural norms and values of the Kirlinos. Truly, at times Caspa could have sworn that Anaka melted

FIGURE 3.2 The ex-coms specialist Anaka.

into their surroundings. Finally, the joy was immense when they truck groundwater.

After a few hours of working together, Caspa felt much closer to the locals, and although he was very happy about the warm welcome, he knew that his chapped hands and overworked arms would make his life hell for the next days. He got to know a dozen people in a very short time, and the initial scepsis turned into honest hospitality. Caspa enjoyed the delicious smelling bread they shared with him, and in early afternoon, Anaka and Caspa retreated into a tent. There were books stacked all over the ground about survival in the desert as well as various human geography and historical treaties about the Kirlinos. Anaka had agreed to the interview and the tiny robot Evali started the recording.

"You are the external communications specialist or called ex-coms in short. The difference to a traditional public relations agent is obvious. You establish a deep connection with the target group, now living here with the Kirlinos and support them with their work. If I may add: I am impressed by your adaptability!"

"My job is all about participatory observation, research and communication, this means I need to be in direct contact with the target group.

Currently I am working on a serious game for the Kirlinos together with our Game Designer Daisy. She just left a few days ago, but I am sure you will meet her soon. The project is supported by a number of international institutions. However, before a system can be designed or developed, I first need to analyse the target group, the context and the space in which the target group will interact with my solution.

"I understand, the ex-coms expert and ideally the entire team should dive into the context. Do the Kirlinos know about your actual agenda?"

"Of course. Before I was allowed to live with them temporally, I made my intentions very clear. I take part in their daily lives as much as possible and learn what is important to them. I talk to people in scheduled interviews but also during work breaks and over dinner. I make use of random, unplanned insights."

"So, you plan for the unplannable? Similar to a serendipity effect, the effect of planned coincidence?"

"It is more than just chance. You actively and intentionally enter situations that have a high probability of generating interesting information. Any information can be relevant to me. I need to obtain information from different sources and contexts. Books, studies, media, questionnaires, interviews, random conversations, observations... The whole range of scientific data generation and collection tools. To maintain an overview, I prepare and structure the analysis phase, despite accepting a momentum of randomness. Let's start at the beginning."

STEP 3.2 SET UP AN ANALYSIS REPORT AND REPOSITORY

The outcome of the analysis phase is the analysis report. Typically, this analysis report is supported by an organized analysis repository. The analysis report summarizes the most important findings from the analysis phase and should also describe where more in-depth information can be found in the analysis repository. The repository usually gets filled by a variety of people, including the game designer, ex-coms or the game director. The repository must be structured in such a way that a new person can quickly find their way around the archive without requiring instructions. The repository contains primary data like interview recordings, sketches, videos of the interaction space, images and audio files, and should also contain secondary data like external reports, studies and market analyses.

I emphasize the importance of an orderly structure, because in a chaotic collection of files, the designer will not be able find the relevant information, which devalues the work of the analysis phase. Why should we collect a lot of data if we can't make use of it? The repository and the report proofs say that we have not blindly developed a game, but have carefully familiarized ourselves with the context beforehand. The analysis report summarizes general information about the project brief and background, the context analysis, interaction space, target group and summarizes further relevant information like external studies. Let's speak about these items in more detail.

STEP 3.3 CONDUCT A CONTEXT ANALYSIS

To gain an understanding of the context, we need to collect a heterogeneity of information, for example information about the natural and geographical aspects of the projects region, dominant cultures, political systems, prevailing religions, history and current developments, networks and systems, internal and external tensions of the region, technical infrastructure and much more. On the one hand, you need to get a holistic overview. On the other hand, you need to select relevant information. We need to decide what information will give us a decisive advantage in designing a successful serious game.

The context is easier to determine if our target group is in a specific geographic region. Country-specific information, literature and human geography treatises are a good source of information to start with, but immersing ourselves in the local context is the best way to obtain authentic and up-to-date information. On site together with the target group, you can shed light on the different aspects of a problem and assess them more realistically. Next to the ex-coms specialist, it is of big added value if at least the game director, the game designer and the artists were able to immerse into the context before they are creating the solution. Even better, having the entire team on board will not only lead to a better understanding of the context and the target group, it will also be a great team building activity that will allow your team to work more efficient on the project, reduce misunderstandings and generate shared experiences in a new context that will increase team bonding massively.

"But what do we do when we create a product that has an extremely diverse target group? For example, when we design a serious game for the employees of an international company or in my case, an international academy? I just saw a fellow student from the academy having problems accessing a simulation, and I am already questioning my initial game approach."

"If you do a proper analysis, your initial approach of the game will change most probably. Try to get an overall picture of the diverse target group. Perhaps you can talk to the different subgroups and observe them in their physical context. Find similarities and differences. At the same time, digital worlds allow us to analyse digital behaviour of the target group. An international company usually tries to establish an organizing corporate culture in their work environment to improve efficiency. Isn't that the same for the academy? Don't get lost or be overwhelmed by this complexity. Think carefully about which information is relevant to you based on the project goals.

Depending on the project, get information about past and current trends. This list can serve as a starting point.

- Natural and geographical aspects of the context, including relevant characteristics of the region like abundance of natural resources or the likelihood of natural disasters and hazards.
- Political system, law systems, health system, relevant economic systems and prosperity of the context.
- Number and demographics of permanent inhabitants, internally displaced people, migrants or people living in a diaspora.
- Dominant cultures, relevant sub-cultures, prevailing religions, ethnic groups, socio-cultural developments, normative systems.
- Cultural awareness and acceptance on ethical topics and inclusion.
- Internal and external tensions, crime rates, conflicts and potential escalations.
- General infrastructure and technical infrastructure, including internet accessibility, access to devices and the gap between urban and rural areas.
- Current pop culture including movies, series, sports, music and arts.
- Predominant analogue and digital gaming trends.
- Relevant aspects regarding the subject matter, for instance existing awareness or preconceptions.

Especially in fragile context, a context analysis contains a risk analysis. The simplest way is the evaluation of events based on two dimensions "probability of occurrence" and "impact on the project."

Caspa scratched his chin: “This reminds me a lot of the stakeholder mapping. The stakeholder has a certain interest which kind of describes the probability of getting active, as well as a potential project impact once getting active as well as a project attitude.”

Anaka nodded: “Correct. However, in the risk analysis, we are not limited to stakeholders, but can list all possible events and activities that pose a risk to the project. Take for example, natural disasters, political conflicts, modifications to analogue or digital infrastructure, the emergence of a new technology of a competitor’s product etc. If the probability is too high for a crucial event and we can’t prepare for it accordingly, the project can be cancelled without causing additional harm.”

STEP 3.4 CONDUCT MARKET RESEARCH

Once you gained general information about the context, you can start scanning the existing market within. Perhaps there are already similar products that you can learn from, perhaps there are competitors to be aware of or potential partners to cooperate with. Especially in development aid, there is most probably another institution or network that is working to find a solution to a similar problem. Unfortunately, I experienced too often “silo thinking” in which institutions with similar targets work on very similar products, sometimes not aware of each other and therefore spending money on the same problem which could be used way more efficiently by partnering. Most of the times this is not the fault of the employees. Cooperation between these institutions are often too complex to establish due to bureaucratic burdens and heavy administrative efforts. This causes institutions to work on the same project in parallel because they can’t follow this bumpy road of bureaucracy while fulfilling their targets. As a consequence, we face competition between the institutions. Sure, competition can also lead to a better quality of products. However, the target group rarely benefits from the situation, facing two average solutions rather than one well developed with a more accurate budget.

If you work in the private sector and face competitors, try to understand their games, learn from their successes and failures and explore if you can find hints of a market niche that you can take into consideration for the design of your serious game. Also scan similar markets that might use other approaches to solve the same problem, for instance other media formats or the traditional training sector. Gaining a holistic overview about the different players in the market and its environment and systems will help you to better define your unique selling propositions. Invest some time in doing market research, there are many studies and reports out there that will reduce your number of assumptions.

STEP 3.5 CONDUCT A TARGET GROUP ANALYSIS

The target group analysis is the most important part of the entire analysis phase. A concept without target group analysis is blind and based on the designer's assumptions. Even if you have been working with the target group for many years or are even part of the target group yourself, a target group analysis should be carried out. We are looking for experiences and stories, we need to understand how our target group works as individuals and as a group.

Let's start with demographic data and the clear definition of the target group. The commissioner usually makes a pre-selection as part of the requirements. I often get blurry target group definitions, for instance "young women from Peru working in the blue-collar labour market." We need to complete this initial demographic description, for instance by asking the question whether the people need to be currently living in Peru, how old they should be and what the meaning of "working" in the blue-collar labour market for the commissioner means.

Reading your impact intention matrix, I see that you defined your target group for your serious game as students enrolled in the academy, which is already pretty good. Market analysis, studies or reports in any form can be relevant for our target group analysis. No new data is generated here, but existing data is examined. It can consist of quantitative and qualitative data. Trusted sources may have already researched and published interest aspects of the target group so we do not have to redo the work done in the past. These studies as well as our context analysis can give us information about a broader group of people within the context, but is not always the same as our target group.

- General demographic information.
- Connection to the context and to other relevant groups within the context.
- Information about education and economic situation.
- Preferences in terms of movies, series, sports, music and arts.
- Literacy, digital literacy and gaming literacy.
- Media Behaviour including the usage of social media and other apps.

- Analogue and digital gaming behaviour.
- Devices and internet accessibility of our target group.
- Dominant game genres and settings, art and sound styles.
- Awareness and knowledge of the subject matter.
- Habits and behaviour related to the subject matter.

This list can serve as a starting point for information you should collect about the target group.

As you can see, some questions from the context analysis and the target group analysis overlap, but the target group within the context might vary from the overarching culture, providing us with interesting insights on motivations or tensions. Let's assume that the predominant pop culture of a context would be classical music. Our target group within this context of classic music lovers prefers rebellious Rock'n'roll music, which provides us with information about their identification, self-understanding and segregation.

Next to desk research, you should also consider setting up questionnaires, especially in case you have direct contact to the target group, for instance employees of a company. You can gain good quantitative and some qualitative data in questionnaires, but interviews will allow to gain the hidden gems of individual stories.

STEP 3.6 CREATE PERSONAS

After gaining a lot of information about the target group, you need to conclude and make it manageable. A persona is a fictitious personality that we created, which serves as a representative of the target group. It tries to bundle as much relevant information as possible. It needs a name, a personal and professional background and a visual representation. Some teams have their persona on a digital board, others print out a picture of the persona and hang it in the team room. You can even make a 3D model of the persona and place it in the workshop room. It may sound exaggerated, but the more present the persona is, the more the designers and artists are reminded in the next phases that they are not designing a solution for themselves (Figure 3.3).

Caspa raised a question: "What happens if our target group is simply too heterogeneous to be summarized in one persona? How do we deal with different genders, ethnic groups or heavily varying age groups?"

FIGURE 3.3 A persona as a permanent reminder.

"A valid question. The answer is the same as with any reduction of complexity: as much reduction as possible, as little as necessary. It often makes sense to represent different genders in different personas, especially if their information, behaviour and attitudes differ significantly. The clearer you can set the focus, the better. If possible, work with one persona. If necessary, work with two or three personas.

STEP 3.7 DEFINE THE INTERACTION SPACE

The interaction space describes the physical or digital room, in which the interaction between the user and the system or game takes place. The situation in which the interaction happens is the use case. The interaction space has a big influence on the use case. Imagine the interaction taking place in a crowded bus or subway and is initiated by the player on a voluntary basis. Now think about an interaction space, in which a user is forced to interact with our game as part of a training, locked up in a school class like environment (Figure 3.4). You can even have an interaction space within another interaction space. Imagine a person with closed VR glasses interacting with other users in a convincing digital waiting room, the primary digital world, and waiting for a training simulation, the secondary digital world, to start. The greater the immersion of the primary digital world, the less influence the analogue world has on the experience.

FIGURE 3.4 The interaction space makes a difference.

Our design needs to be adapted to the interaction space and needs to incorporate the room limitations, but it can also make smart usage of the space properties. When deciding on the intended time of interaction, also called session length, the designer should take the interaction space into consideration. The description of the interaction space should consist of information about the rooms size, conditions, interior, sounds, air quality and also how the user will move and interact with its interior and other people in the space. Is the user alone in the space or can we expect a direct communication between the users? Do we face limitations in internet connection, for instance in a bus ride to a rural area in a development country? Is it likely that my user will mute the sound of the mobile and the game? How long will the user be in the space?

Spaces can be emotionally charged and can have a big influence the individual experience of the user. Do they feel relaxed, safe and happy? Are they anxious, unsecure or even scared? Since we want to convey emotions through our game, the dominant emotional loads of the space help us to design according to the use case.

Let's briefly discuss movie sets remodelled as tourist attractions, as a reference. Visitors link their memories of the movie with their perceptions of the space, which now takes on a completely different meaning and shapes an individual experience, even if the story of the movie is fictional. Depending on the meaning of the movie for the visitor, the fictional scenes of the movie overwrite the real history of the place, at least in the visitor's mind game."

"I've observed that myself. I visited a city where a series was filmed that is very relevant to me. I visited the various filming locations and replayed the fictional moments in the series in my head. For me, the locations served as a gateway to my memories of the fictional story. The fact that the city and the filming locations also had a historical significance in the real world wasn't really important to me, to be honest."

"This is precisely this experience that we can learn from. We need to become aware of the importance of the individual interpretation and the emotional charge of spaces. In design and implementation, we can make use of the existing emotional charge of a space or actively try to enrich a place with an additional layer. In the past, we aimed to draw attention to the historical significance of a world heritage site. We created a digital gaming experience for tourists at this very site before they visit it. We added a thrilling story to the preparatory gaming experience, resulting in a modification of the visitor's later experience on the real site. The player perceived the analogue space with their senses, but interpreted and expanded this perception through their memories and expectations based on the preparatory digital experience (Figure 3.5).

Another approach is the use of existing emotional charges. Think of an analogue space or digital space that might be already very relevant to our players. We trained a global team working on a massively multiplayer online game on the company values, specifically integrity. The training took place in the digital world of the game, at exactly that space where one of the main protagonists of the story was betrayed by her best friend and stabbed. For the target group in this example, a team of developers, this was an emotionally charged space, even if the story was absolutely fictional. The same works for analogue places. Important, international political gatherings often take place in well selected sites with a historical meaning."

"I understand. We can make use of existing emotional charges to support the message of our serious game, or we can intentionally develop emotional charges in order to modify the individual experience of our player."

FIGURE 3.5 Spaces can be emotionally charged.

Anaka would stay a couple of more days with the desert tribe and would follow Caspa to the academy in a few days. Caspa had to do some analysis in the context and interaction space of his project, doing a questionnaire and interviewing as many students as possible. Caspa reflected on his time with the Kirlinos a lot on his flight back, this experience gave him more insights that two years of desktop research. At the same time, he was looking forward to entering the physical academy again, the place he called home for the last five years.

STEP 3.8 PLAY A LOT OF GAMES

Days went by, and Caspa was very busy with the analysis phase, creating a repository and summarizing his findings in the analysis report. The creative director Derren had a guest lecture in the academy, and he could spare some time to support Caspa. The two developers sat together in the centre of the arcade museum of the faculty of gaming history. The museum was filled with old-school pinball machines and retro arcade game machines. Caspa loved strolling around in the dusty corridors of the interactive museum, learning many fun facts about the beginnings of the digital gaming industry. Derren read through Caspa's analysis report, while by a second device, the high concept note was projected as a hologram.

"Derren, while progressing in the analysis phase, I came to the conclusion that my initial game idea might not be suitable for the target group. I thought I knew for whom I was designing, but then I visited the Kirlinos in the desert, observing the fellow students facing problems accessing the digital academy and seeing what kinds of games they play. I am not sure yet, but I think I want to go for a more inclusive approach. Based on their gaming behaviour, I also want to add elements of a rogue-lite game genre, in which the player receives little in-game advantages and carryovers between each run, which represents the capacity building of your team. So, failing one game project is actually not a strict game-over, but offers the possibility to learn and have better chances to be successful in the next run."

Derren smiled: "Lovely, you see how the analysis changes your initial approach and will help you avoid mistakes? As an additional part of your research, you will need to play as many games as possible. Playing games is part of the job. You need to understand what kinds of products are currently out there, what is working with the target group and why. Check out the games they enjoy from all genres, settings and formats, even if you are not enjoying playing this type of game. If you are a developer of digital games, you can learn a lot from analogue games and vice versa (Figure 3. 6).

FIGURE 3.6 Analyse the structure of games.

For professional musicians, it is not easy to just enjoy listening to great music. They tend to have an analysis lens activated, setting a focus on small parts of the entire music composition that a normal listener would not perceive. This is a blessing and curse at the same time and likely will happen to you when you become more experienced in game development. You will not always enjoy the entire experience as a whole, but might examine certain aspects of the game, finding yourself analysing the settings screen and why you actually like it.

You don't always need to reinvent the wheel, so learn from existing games as much as you can. How is the first-time user experience working? Are the motivations of the characters convincing? Are the game loops working and why? In fact, overwhelming your players with too many great innovations might actually make them quit the game, even if your innovations are objectively speaking great. We expect certain things from game genres, these conventions allow us to focus on important and exciting parts of the game and not relearn the basics of movement. Of course you can break with conventions, if it really provides an added value to the experience, but not just for the sake of being innovative. Especially with serious games, we will face the hard challenge to incorporate subject matter into the game loops. We need to become quite innovative anyway. If you already have an idea about your genre and setting, play as many games as possible from this kind, no matter if it is analogue or digital. Of course, you can learn a lot from big AAA games, but there are also many indie game developers out there who really know their stuff."

Caspa was thrilled. Playing games was a part of the development process.

NOTE

1 Please note: The ethnic group of the Kirlinos are purely fictional and not based on real people.

CHAPTER 4

Phase 4

Subject Matter Selection

It was time to get a closer look on the subject matter. For now, Caspa just had a rough overview based on the impact intention, but selecting and prioritizing specific subject matter was a job in itself, and Caspa needed support by an expert.

STEP 4.1 MEET THE SUBJECT MATTER EXPERT

Dr. Sumato was not his favourite teacher at the academy, but she was incredibly knowledgeable. He didn't know any person that knew more about the theory of project management and the process of serious games development. Unfortunately, the practical and interactive part of her lectures were short, she followed an outdated top-down teaching style. That seemed to be the case in many serious games projects, having knowledgeable subject matter experts with little to no understanding of the format of a serious game.

In this case, Dr. Sumato did obviously know about the format of a serious game, but she rarely developed or played them herself. After a couple of days, she invited Caspa to her office, yet library would describe it better. Dr. Sumato had a huge collection of tangible books, which was quite rare given the massive digital library of the academy. The air was a bit musty, dust collected on some thick rolls. There was no service robot around, and after the personal introduction, Dr. Sumato offered Caspa a cup of coffee. She was an aged lady on the verge of retirement and had a slight hump, an

DOI: 10.1201/9781003461531-6

unsteady step, white hair and wore a traditional *magistra magna turban*. Her features showed a certain sternness, and although her body bore witness to her age, watchful and intelligent eyes examined Caspa (Figure 4.1).

FIGURE 4.1 The subject-matter expert Dr. Sumato.

The interview started. Caspa activated his evaluation robot and started with some easy questions to start with. He then steered the interview into the core phase.

"Honorable Dr. Sumato, what makes the role of a subject matter expert and what is subject matter?"

Her voice was thin yet sharp: "Subject matter is the serious content of a serious game. This can be concrete learning content, and can also relate to reflections, reactions or even habit and behaviour change that you want to trigger in your target group. In many projects, subject matter is equivalent to learning content. Even with the raise of artificial intelligence, the human perspective on the subject matter will always play an important role. Having expertise in a subject matter means to connect the dots consisting of knowledge, skills, networks, pitfalls and how the subject matter or learning content should be adapted depending on the target group and context. Ideally, a subject matter expert has also didactical skills, and often it is the task of the game designer to translate the expertise from the subject matter expert into the game experience.

The subject matter expert helps to define subject matter-related goals, so for instance defining reachable learning objectives that are adapted to the current knowledge status of the target group in cooperation with the game director and the game designer. Furthermore, the subject matter expert also supports in the creation of learning material or takes even full responsibility of it. This could mean recording learning videos, writing learning texts or audios and also creating assignments and tests to evaluate the topic-related progress of the target group. Additionally, we want to avoid a sequential learning design, in which the serious content just alternates with the fun experience.

But I am neither a game designer, nor a gamer. Therefore, I need to be in frequent contact with the game designer and support in including the subject matter into the core game loops. The biggest challenge in this exercise is the balance of fun and seriousness. Sometimes, if we want to include too much learning content and going for hyper-realism, this can play against the flow and a fun game experience. Very often, we have to make compromises, reducing learning complexity in the core loops and accepting abstractions. That is why I like to add additional information like traditional texts and videos as exit parts of the game experience, in case the target group wants to dig deeper and gain more detailed knowledge, that can't be handled by the game."

"Wouldn't this be a sequential design? Derren told me to avoid this."

"We try to avoid it, but sometimes there is no way around. If you have very complex learning content, and the limitations of the project budget or simply the game approach wouldn't cover all possibilities, we can either decide to kick out the in-depth learning content or we add it as a deep dive chapter read, for instance. Think about a serious game on mixing cocktails. Due to the limitations of the project, our serious game would teach the player to mix 30 cocktails. As you probably know, there are way more cocktails out there worth spreading." Dr. Sumato winked at him, and Caspa was a bit confused. He didn't expect her to be so… fun.

Caspa reconsidered his first opinion of her, while she continued. "So, what do we do with the remaining 50 cocktails that we would like to teach? The project has not enough budget to afford the artwork, nor implementing it into the game experience. We could just drop the 50 additional cocktails, or we spread the recipes in the game experience as collectibles, replacing insignificant badges and trophies with additional learning content. This brings me to the next important point. You can include complex learning content in a very subtle way, just adapting mechanics in the game. In case you need a currency in your game, do you really need to call it "gold" if your game aims at reconciliation? Couldn't the currency be called "forgiveness" or "respect", adapting also the way this resource is collected? Each aspect of the game and design decision offers an opportunity for learning.

STEP 4.2 PRIORITIZE THE SUBJECT MATTER

The subject matter expert has a lot of experience and knowledge on the topic. It is a challenge to select the right amount of subject matter that should be present in the game. Take the impact intention as a reference and create a subject matter list that prioritizes the different items you want to include. The subject matter expert is responsible for this list and should work closely with the game director on it, communicating it with the commissioner, target group and incorporating the feedback. A subject matter list could be structured like this:

Subject Matter Selection Tool

ID	Name	Learning Target	Type	Sources	Priority	Status
1	Process Overview	Player understands the stages and phases of the and is able to...	Knowledge	Video A Text A Website A	High	Integrated in game version 0.4
2	Application of project steps	Player is able to use and adapt the steps for an own project...	Skill	Video B Text B	Medium	Not integrated yet
3	Multiple use of terms	Player is aware that terms can be used in many different ways and...	Awareness	Text C	Low	Integrated in design document
4	Card Microlearning	Player is encouraged to learn by cards on a daily basis and continues to...	Habit	Video D	Medium	Not integrated yet

This would just be a starting point for your game. Adapt the tool to your needs, but having an overview about the subject matter with linked sources to texts, videos, websites or any other material will help you to come up with a game design that incorporates the serious content in its core and is not just selling the famous chocolate-covered broccoli to the player (Figure 4.2).

FIGURE 4.2 The famous chocolate covered brokkoli.

From an instructional design point of view: Try to develop serious games that encourage self-reflection, the change of habits and behaviour trough the subject matter, rather than simply disseminate learning content. Supporting the player to change one habit will have a significantly higher impact than bombarding them with 100 learning messages. You don't always have the choice, but in case you can incorporate this in your design, you will find out that your impact is way more sustainable, even if it is more indirect.

STEP 4.3 TRAIN YOUR TEAM ON THE SUBJECT MATTER

There is a huge benefit if every team member working on the serious game has a basic knowledge on the subject matter. Along the process, there are limitless big, medium and small decisions done by all members, and even if all big and medium decisions will be discussed in the bigger team, the small decisions in itself have a substantial influence on the shape of the game. And since it is about creating a serious game, the shape of the game should support the serious purpose of it. If the project allows for it, the subject matter expert should train the basics of the subject matter to the team, before the actual game creation starts.

Next to the improvement of the quality of the serious game itself, you will expand the horizon of your team, since a subject matter might be far away from game development. The members might learn aspects that will help the entire team in future projects. Additionally, the job gets way more attractive, if you allow and encourage your team to learn new skills, facts about a variety of subjects or how they can change their habits and behaviour to the better.

These internal trainings can be in the shape of analogue trainings, workshops, webinars, mandatory readings and videos, even of an interactive assignment. The team is required to learn the subject matter, still make it as enjoyable as possible.

STAGE B

Serious Games Creation

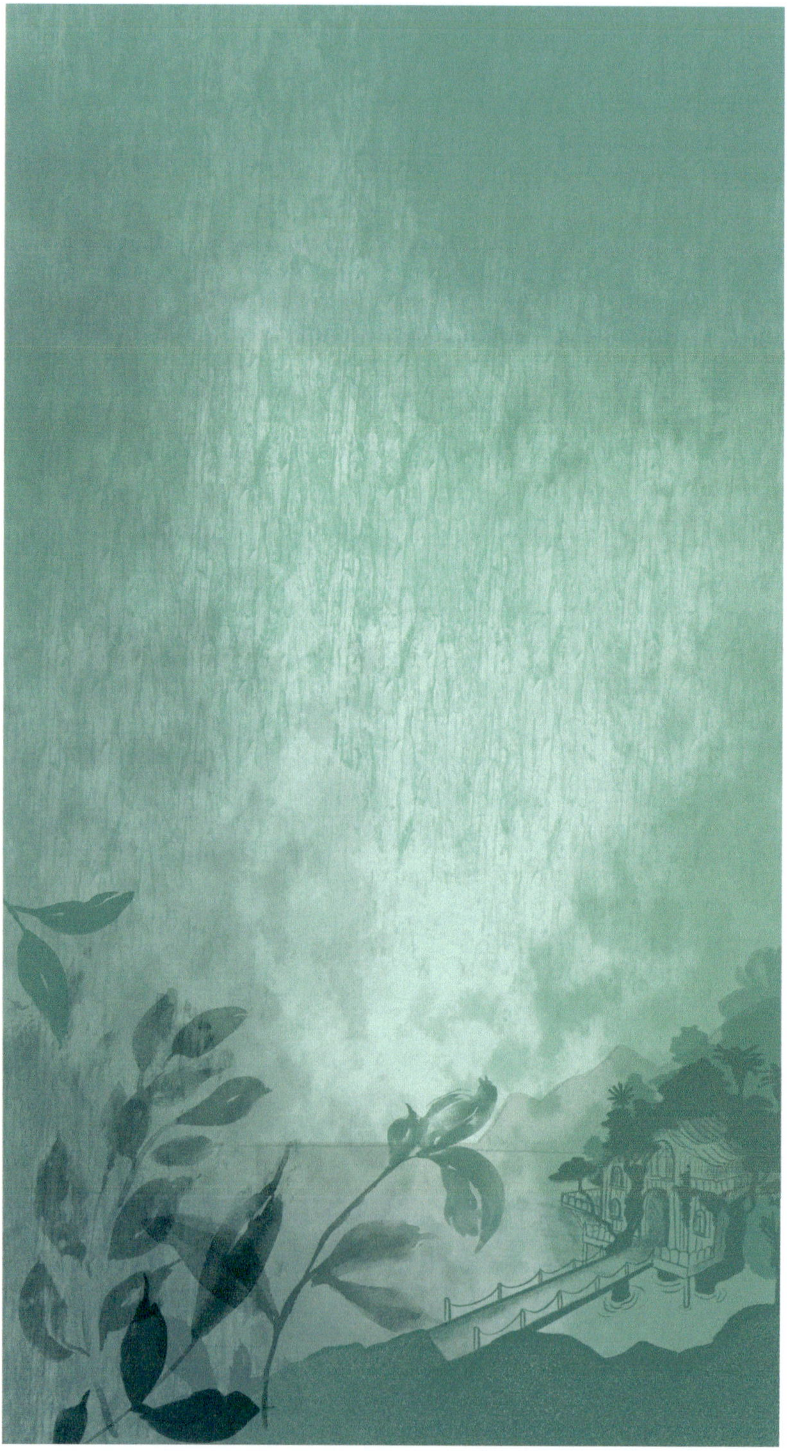

CHAPTER 5

Phase 5

Game Conceptualization

THE WOODEN HOUSE STOOD on stilts in a quite bay with a paradisical view of the open ocean. The waves of the choppy sea were absorbed by the reef in front, with only smaller breakers making their way to the home of the world-famous designer. The house blended naturally into the landscape, and yet it was a colourful work of art in itself. Flowers in every colour of the rainbow flourished in a tropical garden, making their way through the roots of a massive tree that embraced the entire core of the house. Some exotic birds had built their nests under the projections of the balconies, but the most remarkable feature of the house was the impressive roof formed by a wide, colourful tree crown. Numerous aerial roots hung down from the thick branches, some of them reaching the surface of the sea below. Caspa smelled the salt of the sea mingled with a mixture of tropical flowers. The house had been created by man and nature in unison, combining the most beautiful and best ingredients from the surroundings to form a masterpiece of sustainable architecture.

Countless colourful fish and even a few manta rays dove along the walkway, which Caspa now carefully walked on. The old wooden planks creaked under the weight of his shoes, and he was a little worried if the construction, weathered by the sea, would withstand his weight. He smiled and thought: "Trust the process." Reverently, he took step after step forward. Finally at the end of the footbridge, he read the carved inscription above the round front door: Beauty through diversity.

DOI: 10.1201/9781003461531-8

STEP 5.1 MEET THE GAME DESIGNER

Caspa knocked on the wooden door. He stroked his hair nervously and smoothened his clothes. He was about to meet another legend, and even if he already met some of his heroes in the recent past, his gut feeling told him that this person was special. The young developer was about to face the woman whose many ideas had made the world the place it was now. Suddenly a pelican landed on the pier a few metres away from him, but hardly seemed to notice Caspa. Then the door opened and the young developer looked into the face of the most interesting woman he would ever meet.

"Good morning to you! Caspa, I presume?"

Her voice was confident, feminine and extraordinarily harmonious. Long blonde hair framed a remarkable face, her full smile crowned by two dimples. But most mesmerizing were her eyes, one dark and mysterious, the other a bright, extroverted blue (Figure 5.1). Caspa stood there with his mouth hanging open before he caught himself.

FIGURE 5.1 The game designer Daisy.

"It's an honour, Miss Daisy. I am a huge fan, I know about all your work!"

"Please come in and leave out the silly Miss. Just call me Daisy."

The interior of the domicile was not less impressive than the exterior. Lianas, orchids and wonderfully fragrant flowers were omnipresent. Small Gen IV house robots transfused salt water to fresh water and took care of the plants' ideal moisture levels. Caspa saw some of the hand-sized robots symbiotically docking onto a thicker root of the tree to split off a little energy. He smelled a stimulating scent of daffodils emanating from a meditation cove that offered a 360-degree view of nature.

Daisy and Caspa took a seat on the terrace. Daisy closed her laptop, she seemed to be working on some game code. After Caspa introduced himself and explained the project, he asked carefully:

"Could you tell me what is your job as a game designer?"

Daisy took a sip of her tea before explaining. "The game designers are the architects of the game. They need to conceptualize the entire game and integrate the serious content of the game into fun game loops. The game designers went through the analysis of the context and know the target group; they also have solid knowledge on the serious content and are in touch with the subject matter expert. Game designers start with many ideas, then generate quick and dirty prototypes to test specific aspects of the game. They will also include programmers and artists in the process and will be in frequent communication with them, while reporting progress and obstacles to the game director. After a lot of ideation, prototyping and testing, they are responsible to write the game design document (GDD), the blueprint of the game. The game designers are responsible for the gameplay, rules and loops that the game consists of, the controls, the different levels, the story, narrative and worldbuilding, the balancing of the mechanics as well as events and new content when the game is actually online in live operations. Game designers are shaping the experience of the player and are mainly responsible for the fun in the game. But as for serious games, they also need to understand how they can best deliver the serious part of the game to the player, for instance in a learning game making sure that the learning content is an enjoyable and integral aspect of the entire game experience.

Depending on the project, we have additional specializations and own teams working for instance only on the narrative or level design. In smaller developments, all game design responsibilities are taken over by a single game designer, in tiny projects the role of the game designer is taken over by the creative director.

STEP 5.2 CONSIDER RUNNING A HACKATHON OR GAME JAM

To come up with ideas, prototypes and even running games, some commissioners prefer to follow a competitive approach. Hackathons and game jams can be a great way to get a big variety of potential solutions and include local teams in the process. A hackathon is an analogue, digital or hybrid event in which teams compete against each other to come up with a solution on a pre-defined problem. A game jam is a hackathon that is having a game-related outcome. At the end of the event, you might have one or several winners that are funded by the commissioner to continue working on the project (Figure 5.2). We organized hackathons and game jams all over the world, some of them failed horribly, some of them were great successes. Let's consult an expert on this topic."

FIGURE 5.2 A hackathon on healthy oceans with four competing teams.

Daisy turned to Evali: "Please be so kind and play the Mind Games Blink by the fantastic Juliana Brito."

GUEST BLINK JULIANA BRITO, BRAZIL: RUNNING GAME JAMS

Juliana Brito is the CEO and co-founder of Indie Hero and Workay. She is also currently the CEO of GameJamPlus (GJ+), the largest game development marathon in the world focused on business.

The Importance of Game Jams

The game development industry is notably distinct from other economic sectors. This uniqueness can be attributed to its relatively recent emergence, its specific characteristics or its intrinsic peculiarities. Unlike most industries, entering the game development field can be quite challenging, primarily due to a lack of structured internship or trainee programmes. Large companies often prefer hiring senior professionals, leaving few opportunities for juniors. As a result, aspiring developers typically gain experience by working in indie game studios or developing games independently. This trend is especially pronounced in emerging markets like Brazil, where the game development market is still nascent.

In this context, Game Jams play a crucial role for new talents aspiring to enter the game development market. Participating in these events is one of the best strategies for junior developers to build a robust and attractive portfolio. Given the industry's preference for experienced professionals, creating a portfolio through Game Jams becomes indispensable for newcomers seeking visibility and job opportunities.

Beyond portfolio building, Game Jams provide a unique space for practical learning and knowledge exchange. Creating a game within a short period, typically 48 hours, and collaborating with individuals from diverse backgrounds is an enriching experience. These events encourage teamwork and the development of skills beyond one's specialty, which are essential elements of Game Jams.

Moreover, for those wishing to start their own studio, Game Jams are fertile ground for talent discovery and partnership formation. These events bring together people with diverse skills and passions, creating an environment conducive to forming strategic alliances.

Game jams typically last for short periods like 48 hours or 1 week and lack stages for game improvement. One of the most popular global platforms for hosting game jams is itch.io, where anyone can organize events, making it a starting point for many novice game developers. Additionally, in-person game jams, organized by entities like universities or developer associations, remain significant.

Considering the jams held on itch.io, for instance, we can notice that there are various forms of awards, ranging from cash prizes to software subscriptions, engines and asset packages. Winners can be single or multiple, often ranked in top three positions. Awards are commonly given across categories such as art direction and gameplay. For instance, GameJamPlus presents over 15 categories at its ceremony, covering technical, regional and thematic areas, alongside the Game of the Year award.

The Journey of GameJamPlus

GameJamPlus began modestly in 2017, headquartered in a single city. Since then, it has impressively expanded to cover 42 countries and more than 100 cities. Its latest edition saw the participation of 5.000 developers. GameJamPlus transcends mere competition, beginning with a traditional 48-hour hackathon where teams develop game prototypes.

After the initial hackathon, games that show potential proceed to an incubation phase, where they receive mentorship from specialized professionals to enhance their products. The final stage, the acceleration phase, transforms these products into viable businesses. It is essential to know how and to whom to sell the game, how to attract investment and what strategies to employ.

One of the biggest lessons from GJ+ is that success often comes to the most resilient developers rather than those who create the best games. This concept mirrors the world of entrepreneurship, where persistence and adaptability are crucial. The eight-month process of GJ+ tests participants' dedication, and those who remain until the end have a higher chance of success. There have been editions where studios significantly benefited from financial prizes simply for being the only ones to deliver in certain categories. GameJamPlus has contributed to the creation of game studios in at least 20 countries, many of which continue to be active and successful today.

Broader Impact of Game Jams

Game Jams also play a vital role in community building within the game development sector. They bring together developers from around the world, creating a sense of camaraderie and shared purpose. This global connection is not only beneficial for individual developers but also helps in the cross-pollination of ideas, leading to innovative and diverse game concepts.

Additionally, Game Jams often foster the exploration of social and cultural themes in games. By providing a platform for diverse voices and perspectives, these events contribute to the creation of games that reflect a wide range of experiences and stories. This inclusivity helps in making the game industry more representative and varied. In 2018, for instance, GJ+ featured an exclusive category in partnership with UNICEF aimed at developing games to enhance the lives of children in Brazil and worldwide. The winning game, One Dollar, addressed sustainability and water conservation issues.

Another significant aspect of Game Jams is their contribution to technological advancement. Developers frequently experiment with new tools, engines and technologies during these events, leading to breakthroughs that can influence the broader industry.

Conclusion

Participating in Game Jams offers invaluable opportunities for junior developers and aspiring entrepreneurs. These events facilitate the creation of impressive portfolios, promote networking, mutual collaboration and professional growth. Game Jams are not just competitions; they are catalysts for innovation and development. They provide a dynamic and creative environment where developers can explore their capabilities, learn new skills and form valuable connections, making them essential for the flourishing of the game industry.

STEP 5.3 RESHAPE THE INITIAL APPROACH

You can either work with the winning teams from the game jams or you skip the game jams and just go with your own team. In the past, we also combined the approaches, collaborating with local teams that won a game jam and support our development team with local expertise.

No matter if you run a game jam or if you work by yourself, the start of the game conceptualization phase is determined by the magnificence of ideation. Even if we had an initial game shape in the pre-creation stage, the new insights gained in the analysis phase will require us to reflect on our initial approach (Figure 5.3). Our commissioner should be aware that the shape might change throughout the process, and now it is the time. We want to create a solution that is based on evidence, not assumptions.

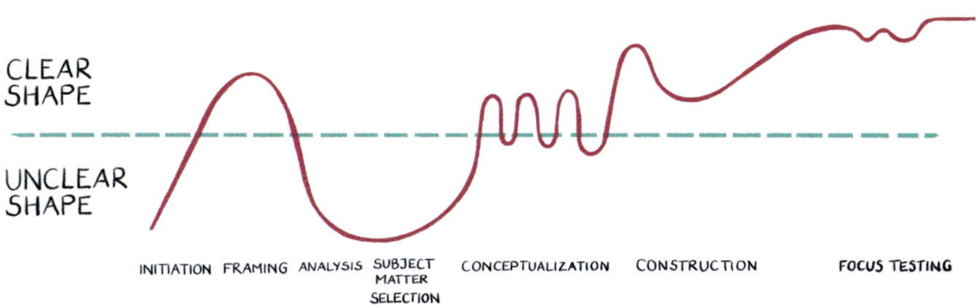

FIGURE 5.3 The game shape variation curve.

To start, we need to go for quantity and generate as many ideas as possible. Then we select, adapt and merge the most promising ideas that will further define our game concept. First of all, it is important to understand that we cannot "make" creativity. We can just actively create the right circumstances that make it easier for us to work creatively or that creativity can unfold. A creative ideation process is wild, breaks rules and is difficult to control. And that's why I love it.

One of the best possibilities to foster creative co-creation is to organize game design workshops.

STEP 5.4 CONDUCT A GAME DESIGN WORKSHOP

Game design is a process of co-creation. We are in frequent contact with a heterogeneous team and the target group. Running a game design workshop (GDW) is a good way to initiate the game creation stage and bringing all stakeholders up to speed, following a participatory approach (Figure 5.4). I like to run GDWs with a duration of two to three full days. Purely digital GDWs need to be adapted in time, usually I am going for four-hour sessions for two to three days. It is important to have a night in between, allowing our brain to process information and inspirations. Very often, the best ideas arise in the morning of the second day.

The GDW is an essential point in the process. Generating ideas together will not only inspire the team spirit; it will also reduce the miscommunication of the game's vision once the construction phase starts. Perhaps most importantly, the participation in the creative process will increase the ownership of all involved people, making the project their baby. They will feel appreciated and intrinsically motivated to contribute to the project, allowing for self-realization while being part of a bigger team. This doesn't mean that you need to include every single idea, but make use of the collective intelligence, harvest ideas and then afterwards conclude and adapt them into a working concept."

"Got it. Who should be part of the GDW?"

"Based on your team size, you can either invite the entire development team or just one or two representatives of each role. I try to avoid having more than 15 people in permanent presence. Sometimes, people just participate in parts of the workshop, which is acceptable, but make sure to have enough buy-in to stimulate the team spirit."

"If ownership and clear communication structures are important outcomes of the workshop, shouldn't we also invite the commissioner and the target group to participate in the workshop?"

FIGURE 5.4 Co-creation in a Game Design Workshop.

"The answer is not trivial. Let's start with the commissioner. One option is to have the commissioner included in certain parts of the workshop, especially if there is a digital component to the workshop. Of course, it is of a huge added value if the commissioner feels a good amount of ownership to the project. Very often, they want to be part of the GDW to steer it into the direction they envisioned, which is understandable since they want to minimize the risk of a bad invest. On the other hand, having the commissioner on board can come along with certain risks. At first, there might be a problem of hierarchy, making the opinion of the commissioner more important than anybody else of the team. I myself was commissioner in many GDWs at the beginning of my career, and reflecting on it my ideas had too much weight because people didn't want to upset me. It manipulates the creative process making participants hesitant sharing their own ideas, reducing the quality of the creative outcome.

Finally, the commissioner is not always a game development expert, and while they should trust the team and the process, they tend to set too much focus on the subject matter, forgetting the importance of a fun experience. After the GDW happened, the game designer adapts and kicks out ideas from the GDW. The game designer might be hesitant to kick out a bad idea from the commissioner, resulting in a bad design. On the other hand, the commissioner might be upset that their favourite aspect of the game they came up with was erased further down the path. I once experienced that "killing the darling" of the commissioner, their favourite idea, caused a serious conflict. I remember the commissioner saying: "But I wanted it like this and you all confirmed that it was a good idea. I am paying for it, so get it done as agreed."

Regarding the involvement of the target group, we face a similar problem. Since we know that we are developing a game for our target group, their ideas, feedback and voice might be given too much weight in the process. I participated in many workshops in which the wrong decision was made by just accepting the voice of the target group dogmatically: "The target group wants it like that." A killer argument, which should be used very carefully.

Also, if just a few people from the target group take part in the workshop, you can't get a representative picture of the entire mass. Furthermore, the target group doesn't always know what they really want or how game design works. This said, it can be incredibly valuable to have feedback and ideas from the target group, but reflect on it and carefully integrate it into the design. Usually, I advise people to not have the target group present in the entire workshop, but rather test certain prototypes or ideas with them in separate sessions, or running isolated ideation sessions with them to not stifle the creativity and expertise of your team.

My statements on the participation of the commissioner and target group are valid not only for the GDW, but for the entire conceptualization. Incorporate their ideas and feedback, maintain a clear and transparent communication and make sure to select the best ideas for the right reasons."

"Understood. Going back to the GDW, can you summarize what we do and what could be an outcome?"

"Next to improving the team spirit, you should generate as many ideas as possible, really go for quantity. You want to foster collaborative creativity, which is a lot of fun and very demanding. Ideation requires a trusting and open atmosphere, the participants reveal something intimate about themselves, similar to an artist, they give insights into their unfiltered thoughts and most abstruse ideas. Ideation in general, but especially the collaborative creativity, requires a "Yes, and…" mindset. Similar to an improvisational theatre, we accept every stimulus from our peer and build on the idea of the other person without judgement to unleash the full potential of the group. Any idea, no matter how absurd, can trigger a meaningful idea in another person, so the absurd idea can be just as important as the "meaningful" idea.

Note down all ideas and be as visual as possible. Later in the process, you can select the best approaches, merge and adapt them. You can discuss about the narrative, characters and game rules, mechanics and loops. You can select ideas, decide on a genre and setting, build and test prototypes, construct concept art and even initial code. Have an experienced moderator who is able to guide you through the workshop, either the creative director or an external person. This means you can do a lot of steps of the conceptualization phase in the GDW itself. Depending on the available time, it can happen that you just end with many ideas, which is also fine. I will explain the certain steps in more detail, whereby it is not important whether you carry them out in the GDW or afterwards.

STEP 5.5 DECIDE ON A GENRE AND SETTING

Having a tentative genre and setting at the very beginning of the process in the high concept note is often required to make the game tangible and allowing for a better communication with external stakeholders. However, throughout the process, we might realize that we could achieve our targets way better if we change the initial genre and setting. This might result from getting a deeper understanding of the context and the target group, changing requirements or we just had a better idea in the ideation process. No matter what, we need to inform and agree with the commissioner on these substantial changes.

The genre of a serious game describes how the game is played. It is a categorization of games based on their mechanics and gameplay, for instance role play games, strategy games, shooter games, racing games, puzzle games, etc. The genres have certain conventions how the player interacts with the game, for example how they control a character. One game can have several genres, for instance a real-time strategy game blended with a puzzle game.

The setting of a serious game is the time, geographic location and the approach of the story, either fictional or non-fictional, similar to a movie. Famous game settings are for instance medieval fantasy worlds, historic wild west settings, realistic present time cities, near future science fiction spaceship, parallel dystopian universe in the far future, etc.

The choice of the genre and setting should serve the purpose of the serious game. A utopian near future setting might be a good choice for supporting a change process of a company towards sustainability, while a mystical fantasy world could be a good pick for an educational game for kids raising awareness on the consequences of digital bullying. As you can see, some choices are more obvious than others, but be open to explore the advantages of each of the options. Keep in mind the context, target group and especially the impact intention. Experiment with certain genres and settings and always gather feedback from your target audience.

From my experience, the commissioner wants to have a big say on the setting. People who are not in the gaming industry usually care less about the genre, and the setting is important since it easily forms a picture in a person's mind. They will need to communicate the game to their colleagues and superiors and have to feel comfortable with it. Imagine a company is funding a serious game on teamwork. The company culture is highly competitive, conservative and always wants to be one step ahead of their competitors. Therefore, a "knights and dragons fantasy" setting could be the wrong choice, since the employees might devalue the game as "childish and not fitting their vision" just because of the setting, no matter how good the game actually would be when playing. Therefore, make sure that your commissioner agrees or even choses the setting from a pre-selection. This will increase ownership and make communication and implementation way easier.

STEP 5.6 IDENTIFY YOUR GAME LOOPS

The gameplay describes the way in which players interact with the game and is often roughly pre-defined by the selected genre, for instance an "endless-runner" approach. However, the genre is just a categorization and makes use of conventions to improve the communication and onboarding process of a player. The coreplay is the heart of the gameplay. It summarizes the most important game loops and game mechanics that have a big influence on the game experience.

A game loop in game design is the recurring game interaction that your player will do over and over again. In most games there is one or two dominant loops, also called core game loops. These core game loops can form the coreplay, and can also be supported by a major game aspect that is not in the shape of a loop, for instance a ticking timer. Most game loops consist of a performance, targets and obstacles. The performance is the activity that the player is doing to achieve the target. The target is a desirable state of the system. The obstacle is what challenges the player who wants to achieve the target. It could be an enemy in the game, another player or general limitations of the rules of the game. Think of a jump and run game that mainly consists of collecting gold nuggets which are hard to reach.

Going a bit more into detail, a game loop is often supported by a trigger, mind game, change of states, feedback and reflection. The trigger can be a systematic trigger, a co-player trigger or an internal trigger that emerges from the player itself. The trigger reminds us that we could or have to perform the game loop and therefore stimulates activity. Trigger can be very explicit and direct, like a character pointing in a direction saying "Go there now!" or implicit and a bit hidden, for instance a subtle glow on a collectible item.

The mind game is the cognitive process that happens inside the players head, perceiving and interpreting the trigger, matching it with desired targets and a status quo of the game values, elaborating different strategies and roughly calculating their success rate, an expectation of the outcome and a decision for a performance. This mind game often takes less than a second.

Then the performance takes place and the game compares the quality of the performance with the difficulty and the values of the obstacles. This leads to a change of states, for instance when the player collected a coin and the savings go +1. Here, the impact measurement systems also kick in and collect pre-defined in-game data.

In the feedback stage, defined parts of the change of states are communicated to the player, for instance a big "+1" on top of the avatars head. The player will match the feedback with their outcome expectation in the first mind game and now do a reflection on their performance as well as an elaboration on the system, for instance if the game is perceived as "fair." This reflection phase is where the learning takes place, based on the reaction of the system and therefore should be carefully designed for serious games. Next time the trigger will appear, the performance of the player might change based on the learnings from the last loop process (Figure 5.5).

STEP 5.7 SPRINKLE PIXIE DUST

I like to share the secret ingredient that I call pixie dust. I try to add it to all my games. Many people seek for immersion, escapism or something that is a bit supernatural. Technological advancement and science tend to communicate a disenchantment of the world. But we humans want to get enchanted, we want to play with our creativity and expand our horizon.

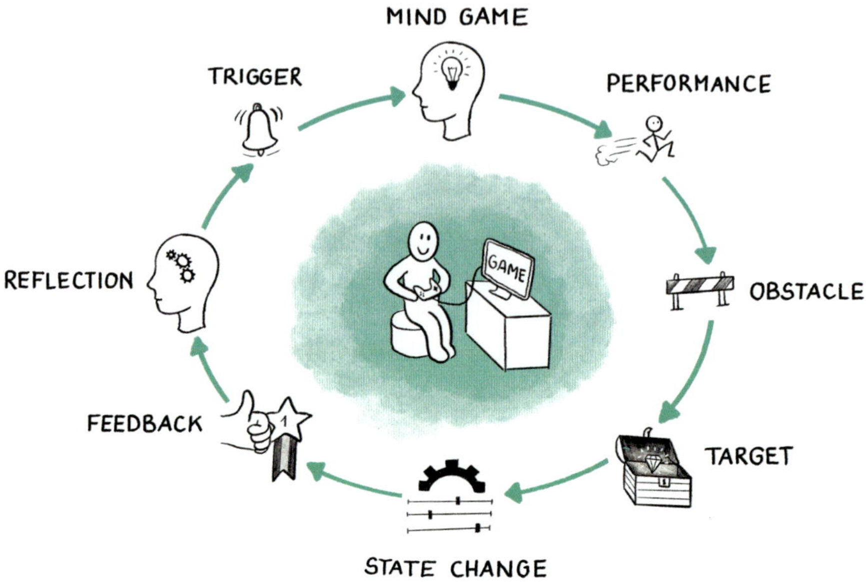

FIGURE 5.5 A potential serious game loop.

Even if you create a serious game for serious people, this doesn't mean that your narrative can not have a little pixie dust, enriching the reality with some "magic." Next to making the learning more interesting, this approach can actually support the player to break up and rewire existing thinking patterns, making the interaction with the subject matter more memorable and connecting it to an individual mind game that is unique for each player. It also justifies abstraction, since the player understands that the game is not "super-realistic" and can integrate all eventualities of reality. Pixie dust helps to remind the player that they are playing a game, which doesn't mean that this would reduce their learning outcome. It communicates that the player needs to extract the subject matter from the game and adapt it to their real environments, allowing for a more individual learning experience (Figure 5.6).

Pixie dust is often communicated via a narrative. The narrative is an essential aspect of most serious games and a great way to communicate the relevance of the subject matter to the player. There is a brilliant Mind Games Blink on the power of narrative. Evali, please play the video of the terrific Paul Darvasi."

FIGURE 5.6 Pixie dust as the magical ingredient of serious games.

GUEST BLINK PAUL DARVASI PHD, CANADA: THE POWER OF NARRATIVE IN SERIOUS GAMES

Paul Darvasi is a game designer and researcher who works at the intersections of games, learning, social impact and culture. He is the CEO of Gold Bug Interactive, the Executive Director of the Serious Play Conference, and he lectures at the University of Toronto.

Storytelling is as old as humanity itself. From ancient myths passed down through generations to the modern narratives we consume in books, films and games, stories have always been a fundamental way for us to make sense of the world. They shape our understanding, convey values and connect us emotionally to different experiences. In the realm of serious game design, the importance of narrative cannot be overstated. It is the narrative that transforms a game from a mere sequence of actions into a meaningful and engaging experience.

In any game, the primary goal is to engage the player. This engagement is particularly critical in serious games, where the objective often extends beyond entertainment to include education, training or social impact.

Narrative serves as the heartbeat of this engagement. A well-crafted story captivates players, drawing them into the game world and encouraging them to invest emotionally in the outcome.

Consider the game Assassin's Creed: Origins, which is an entertainment game that has been used to teach history. It presents factual information in an interactive format, and it is the narrative – woven through the eyes of Bayek, a Medjay in ancient Egypt – that makes players retain the information and understand its relevance. The narrative provides context and significance, making the learning experience both memorable and impactful.

One of the most profound effects of narrative in serious games is its ability to forge emotional connections. When players identify with characters or become invested in a story, they experience empathy, curiosity and a range of emotions that enhance their engagement. These emotional connections are not just fleeting feelings; they can lead to deeper reflections and understanding.

For instance, in This War of Mine, a game designed to address social issues, the narrative is a powerful tool to foster empathy. It tells the story of civilians struggling to survive in a war-torn city, helping players understand the complexities and challenges faced by real people in similar situations. By stepping into the shoes of these civilians, players develop a more nuanced perspective on the issue, which can lead to greater empathy and, potentially, action in the real world.

Narrative also serves as a guide for the player experience, providing direction and motivation. In the absence of a story, players might find themselves aimlessly navigating the game world. A well-structured narrative gives purpose to their actions, leading them through the game in a coherent and satisfying manner.

This is particularly important in serious games where the learning objectives or messages must be clear and coherent. For example, in Kerbal Space Programme, a game designed to teach scientific concepts, the narrative can present challenges and puzzles that align with the educational content. The story guides players through these challenges, ensuring that the educational objectives are met in an engaging and structured way.

The integration of narrative in serious games also enhances the retention and transfer of knowledge. Studies have shown that information presented within a narrative context is more likely to be remembered and applied in different contexts.[1] This is because stories provide a framework for organizing information, making it easier to recall and relate to existing knowledge.

Crafting compelling narratives for serious games requires a careful balance between storytelling and game mechanics. The narrative should be seamlessly integrated into the gameplay, enhancing rather than overshadowing it. This involves creating believable characters, constructing engaging plots and building immersive worlds that resonate with players.

Moreover, the narrative should be flexible enough to accommodate player choices and actions. Interactive storytelling allows players to influence the course of the story, creating a sense of agency and personal investment. This interactivity is a defining feature of games as a medium and should be leveraged to its full potential in serious game design.

Conclusion

The importance of narrative in serious game design cannot be overstated. It is the narrative that transforms a game from a mere collection of mechanics into a rich, engaging experience that resonates with players on an emotional and intellectual level. As serious game designers, we must harness the power of storytelling to create games that not only entertain but also educate, inspire and drive meaningful change.

By weaving compelling stories into the fabric of our games, we aim to create experiences that are not only enjoyable but also transformative, leaving a lasting impression on players long after they have put down the controller.

STEP 5.8 HANDLE EXPECTATIONS OF THE COMMISSIONER

In serious games, we should embed the subject matter into all aspects of the game experience. As Dr. Sumato mentioned, a sequential design should be avoided. Players understand quickly when a game offers boring learning lessons that are interrupted by fun game moments. Playing a jump and run game which is disrupted by unrelated math lessons is probably not the best serious game design. Unfortunately, these explicit learning interruptions are appreciated by many commissioners, because they paid for a "serious" game and can clearly spot the subject matter. This is especially true in development aid, for instance when a minister plays a serious game at a conference for 60 seconds and reaches the explicit math lesson in the game. If this lesson would be hidden and integrated thoughtfully into the core loop, the minister would probably not see the learning content directly and would question the approach of investing tax money in games."

"I see the problem. In this example, we somehow have two target groups. The main target group consisting of kids and another one that is a commissioner who is not familiar with serious game design. How do you satisfy both of them?"

"Not an easy question. In a perfect world we should just focus on satisfying our main target group and convince the commissioner with great

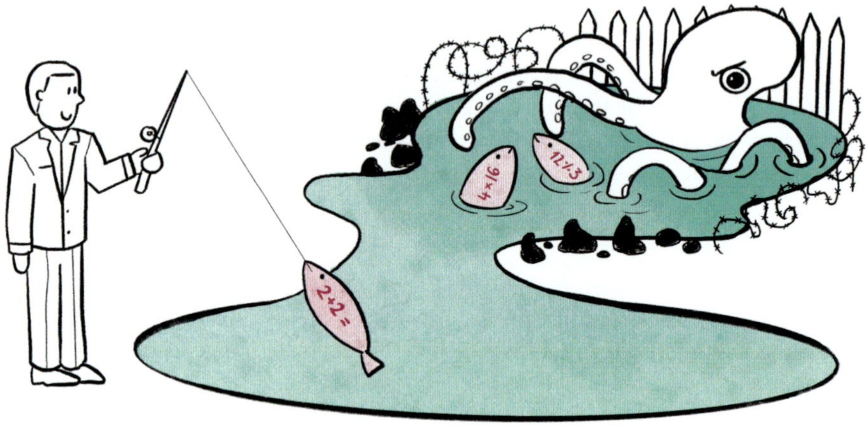

FIGURE 5.7 The early catch satisfies the commissioner.

data from our impact measurement systems. In reality, the commissioner often wants the learning content more explicit and in a traditional style. Here I sometimes use a trick which I call the early catch (Figure 5.7). In the first 60 seconds of gameplay, I try to add one very explicit subject matter element. For instance, in the intro of a game on human rights, the player could collect an ancient stone tablet with the first human right engraved. Usually, you would probably reward the player with this tablet after finishing the first boss fight in order to increase the perceived value of the tablet, but in this case, we want our commissioner or minister who plays the game for 60 seconds to see that learning about human rights is a central part of the game experience.

STEP 5.9 DESIGN YOUR MAGIC CIRCLE

Most serious games make use of the magic circle, a protected learning environment in which the player is allowed to interact with the game without having direct consequences in the real world. I use this circle as part of a journey and enrich it with meaningful subject matter interactions that are inspired by the self-determination theory,[2] explaining the importance of autonomy, competence and relatedness for intrinsic motivation. Remember that the experience happens in the players mind and is just directed by tangible and non-tangible stimulations by the game.

The journey starts with a promise. Our game promises either fun, interaction with the subject matter or ideally a mixture of both. The game should communicate the relevance of the subject matter and how it connects to existing knowledge of the player.

This brings us to contextualization and to enable the player to link the learning content to existing knowledge. When entering the magic circle, the game recognizes the status of the player and adapts the magic circle accordingly. The learning motivation is increased when the player understands that they can link the subject matter to their existent knowledge. We can make use of the flow principle, neither over- nor underchallenging the player. If we adapt the subject matter to the learner's context, the person can process the learning content more easily, better memorize it and build solid neuronal connections. The author Celia Hodent[3] describes the importance of interactivity, relevance and contextualization for learning in games.

Relevance is one of the most important motivations for learning and is connected to a purpose. We can distinguish between two types of relevance: the in-game relevance and the out-game relevance. If the player wants to progress in the game, the player must learn and improve their actions in order to overcome the obstacles, which would correspond to in-game relevance. Very often, a narrative is used to communicate the in-game relevance.

The out-game relevance promises the player that the skills they have just learned or that the interaction with subject matter is also relevant outside the game world. Communicating the out-game relevance is a design decision. Sometimes it is elegant to withhold this information so as not to take players out of the immersion of the game. At a certain point, it is then communicated what relevance the acquired skills have outside the game. You can also communicate the relevance directly, which can increase the players motivation during the experience.

The decisions of the player in the game should matter. They can learn by trying out to be someone else, exploring the consequences of different ways of behaviour, actions or decisions. How does it feel to be the bad guy? How is the environment reacting to me? In the real world, trying out a different personality would quickly lead to serious consequences. This is also true if there are other human players in the game. Being a bully in the digital world has direct consequences to other players, which unfortunately is often witnessed in anonymous digital worlds. Nonetheless, if the experience is well designed, the player can learn and explore through autonomous decisions, driven by curiosity.

Designing an interactive game loop that entertains players in the long term is a challenge in itself. Weaving in subject matter is the fine art of serious game design. The subject matter must naturally fit into the game, the challenges of the game should give the players the feeling that mastering the subject matter content leads to progression within the game and is therefore relevant. The player can try and fail, fail again and eventually get better until they overcome the challenge, making the accomplishment meaningful. This path to mastery encourages learning through failing.

In multiplayer games, recognition by the group for defeating an opposing player plays Ú significant role, depending on the game's design and the player's motivations. The designer tries to link the subject matter with the social interactions between players in the game. This social driver can even kick in when playing a single player game. When the subject matter promises an impact on social interaction outside of the game, it makes use of the same motivational social driver, shaping the players mind game to a fictitious social interaction while playing a single player game.

Every interaction in the magic circle can be tracked and evaluated. At first this sounds great for impact measurement. However, if the player has the feeling that everything they are doing will cause consequences, for instance getting a promotion or getting fired, a lot of learning potential is

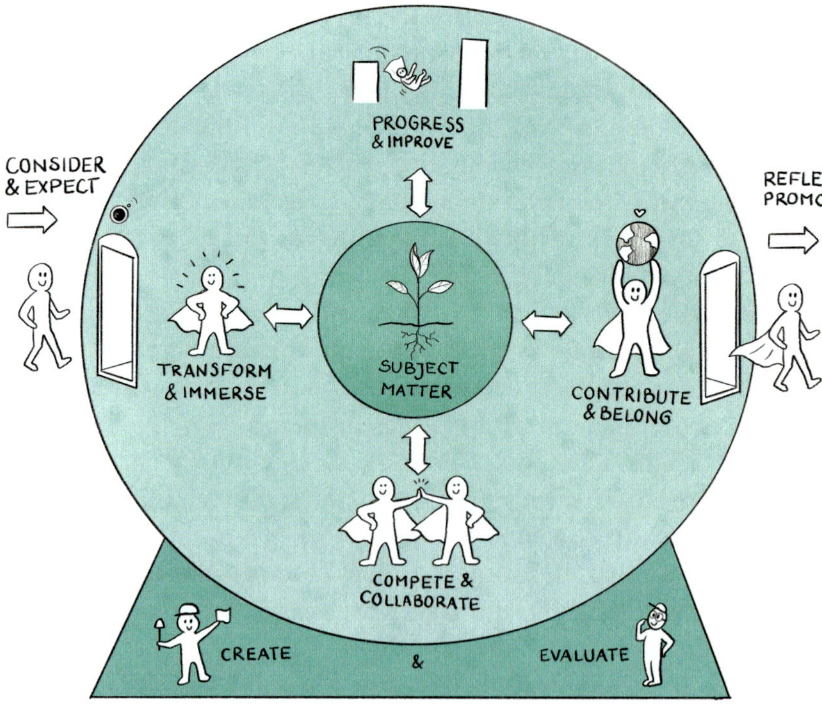

FIGURE 5.8 The serious games sphere.

taken away from the serious game, and it is not different to a test or assignment anymore. Carefully decide what kind of data you track and communicate it transparently to your player. Of course, you can also think about two circles: One training circle where no data is collected and the player can do whatever they want, and another circle in which their performance is evaluated".

Caspa summarized: "We perform in a protected learning environment and afterwards transfer the learnings from the magic circle into the real world" (Figure 5.8).

STEP 5.10 BE AWARE OF THE ILLUSION OF FREEDOM

During lunch, Evali was sitting on Caspa's shoulder, making itself known by pulling lightly on the lobe of his ear. Caspa patted it gently on the head. He somehow felt really close to that cute robot.

Daisy smiled, and Caspa got lost in her eyes. She began to speak: "The empathy update seems to be working well on you. You know that it is actually a team of designers that you are petting, right?"

Caspa stopped his action and turned to Daisy: "What do you mean?"

"Well, no matter if it is a homunculus or if we talk about serious games. The game designer is the one that pre-designed your experience. They take you by the hand, even without you recognizing it. Actually, it is something we have to be aware of while designing games. We as designers are influenced by the outer world, or the reality, as well as we have an impact on the reality. So has the player. However, while designing a game world and decide what actions will be rewarded in the game, we have an indirect influence on the player. This manipulation causes an indirect change of reality via the player. The player might behave differently after playing the game, either for the good or bad.

Also, the game as an artefact changes the reality per se and also can get influenced by the reality, for instance if it works with live data from the real world. But the most important point I want to make is the following: We as game designers are influenced by our environment. We then design games that can serve as an instrument to manipulate players. These players can then again serve as an instrument to change reality by acting in a way that we intended, without knowing our agenda or that we actually exist. Even if you as a player think that you can freely move in a digital world and have total control, everything is pre-designed by us. The perceived freedom of choice in game environments is an illusion that all players should be aware of" (Figure 5.9).

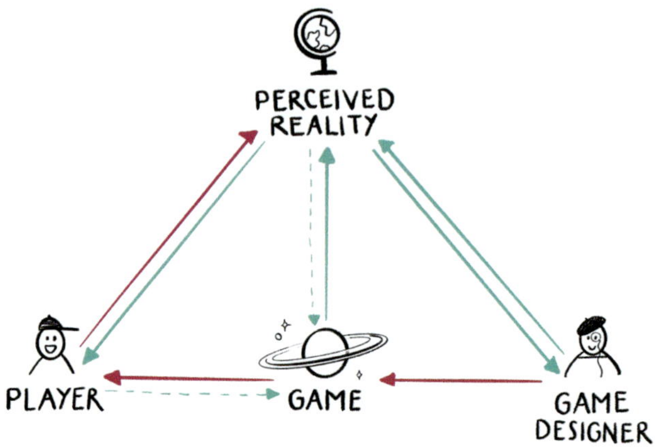

FIGURE 5.9 The indirect manipulation of the player.

Caspa reflected on it and was somehow frightened: "A serious game is a powerful tool, and just as a hammer you can use it to build a house or smash a head."

STEP 5.11 DESIGN FOR INCLUSION

The pelican nearby grabbed a fish from the water and flew over the jetty. The fish wriggled and escaped from its beak, then fell onto the terrace. Evali made a surprised sound, causing Caspa and Daisy to laugh. Daisy looked for a moment at the fish on dry land. It was a very quick one in the water, but on the land, it was totally helpless. She then lovingly picked it up and threw it back into the sea.

"Have you thought about an inclusive design in your game? There is a great Mind Games Blink by the brilliant Dr. Kat Schrier. Let's listen and learn from her." Daisy nodded in Evali's direction and the video began.

GUEST BLINK DR. KAT SCHRIER, USA: INCLUSION IN GAMES

Dr. Karen (Kat) Schrier is Full Professor and Director of Games & Emerging Media at Marist. She is also a game design consultant for World Health Organization (WHO) and CEO of PlatyPlay, LLC, which designs games for care, health, and inclusion. Dr. Schrier is the author/editor of over 100 published works, including We the Gamers (Oxford University Press) and Knowledge Games (JHU Press). She has over 20 years of experience in game development and has worked for Nickelodeon, Scholastic and BrainPOP.

In My Five Moments: The Game, a game to teach the World Health Organization (WHO)'s My Five Moments of Hand Hygiene, we needed to show the game players where the patient and healthcare zones are located. This includes determining which colours to use for each zone. It needed to show up against the alien world-inspired clinical settings, but it also needed to show up for players with all different types of visual abilities. To consider this, we created a chart of how each colour would look for different colour blindness (including blue-yellow and red-green). Likewise, we thought about how to design for other types of accessibility, like having two different game control systems (buttons for hand hygiene stations) and multiple types of scaffolding and feedback (task list, text-based feedback, visual animations, audio noises). We also thought about inclusion in terms of translation and will be translating our game to the six official UN languages.

It is, however, easier said than done. We made a list of all the types of accessibility features we wanted to include, but due to time constraints, as well as technological constraints, we could not include every feature we wanted. For instance, we wanted to include the ability for screen readers to read aloud the text in the game and describe all the visuals, but this can be tricky in a 3D game with animations of aliens in them. Likewise, we wanted our game to be able to be run in low-bandwidth areas, but including audio or animations in it can quickly increase the size of the game. Accessibility and inclusion should be prioritized from the start, rather than being plopped on after the fact. This makes for a better learning experience, and also a smoother design and production process. It means that you can budget for inclusion from the start, rather than having to find the budget later on.

Inclusion does not just relate to enhancing who can play and where they can play, it is also about who is empowered to design the game. Games should not just represent different types of people and cultures, but it should ensure that people from those cultures are able to tell their own stories and share their own backgrounds. This makes those stories more authentic, and it also ensures that the design is more robust. Even in games that are not about cultures or do not include characters, having more voices and approaches to design helps to create a more inclusive learning experience. It means that we can better advocate for different learners. For instance, I am working with a team in India to design games for social and emotional learning (SEL) for rural Indian children. To do this, we are working with Indian researchers and the children to co-design the activity. I also worked with a team in Nigeria (Lagos Business School) and Nigerian youth to co-create a VR game for Nigerian teenagers to practise empathy for different ethnicities there. Neither of these games should be made solely by me (a designer in New York); but rather, they should be co-developed in a way that the learners themselves are empowered to show us how they learn and how they want to play.

Just like we might need to test designing a fun game and an accurate representation of a topic or skill, we also need to constantly test the game and find the best balance to design for inclusion and accessibility. Continuous testing and improvement are key components of the design process. Designers will want to make sure that the game is meeting its learning objectives, and that it is also connecting with the target audiences and enabling access. Designers should seek to test with audience members with all different abilities, backgrounds, learning needs and interests. They should listen to the players and treat them as equal partners in the process, rather than being defensive or dismissive. Players should be encouraged to "break the game" and designers should listen to see how to update everything from navigation to characters to colour schemes so the game is more accessible. Throughout the design process, designers may want to ask questions like:

1. Who has agency in the game? Who has agency over the game's design?
2. How do the choices that players make in a game affect who is included or excluded?
3. How might players learn from their mistakes? What happens if learners engage in problematic behaviour like hate speech?
4. How do we reward positive communication, connection and care?
5. How are we enabling culturally sensitive communication?
6. What types of accessibility features are we prioritizing and how do we ensure these features are integrated into the whole design process?
7. How are we pushing players safely outside of their comfort zones?
8. When can players "break the rules" or break with norms or conventions?
9. Who benefits (or does not benefit) from the game's rules and other aspects of the design?
10. What types of policies are being used and valued? How are players protected and included in the policies and policy-creation?
11. If it is a multiplayer game, how is conflict being managed? How are friendships able to form?
12. How are we avoiding stereotypical representations of people?
13. How do we avoid problematic types of role-playing, such as role-playing as oppressors?

14. Are sensitivity readers and diversity consultants being included and empowered? How can they be not just evaluating the work but an integral part of the design team?
15. How are players allowed to express their full identities and bring their full selves to the game (and see their full selves included in the design of the game)?
16. Who might or might not feel like they belong in the game?

Conclusion

The most important thing is to prioritize belonging, care and inclusion throughout the process. Inclusion should never be an add-on at the end, but it should be an important aspect of the design – how you design, who can design and what you design.

STEP 5.12 MEET THE GAME ARTISTS

Daisy invited Caspa on a short sailing trip to meet their friends Panita and Sondu. The two artists were friends living together on a boat and spent the winter on the archipelago. The group wanted to go for a campfire night by the sea and planned to sleep in the open air. After a scenic crossing through the bay in the afternoon, the small sailboat glided onto the sand of the small neighbouring island. Caspa saw an athletic man sitting in front of a small campfire, an acoustic guitar in his hands and headphones around his neck. His dark voice rose: "Sweet tone, Daisy. Can you take your boat to the coast again and I'll record the scratching?" Sondu laughed and helped Daisy secure the boat, while Caspa felt a little lost. After a warm greeting, the sound engineer pointed to a silhouette. "Panita is over there, can you go get her while we take care of the boat? She's a little dreamer, don't be afraid to wake her up!"

Panita was capturing the sunset on the sea on an easel. At least that's what Caspa thought she was doing, and when he carefully approached her, he realized that she was just using the scenery as inspiration. On her digital easel was a moving avatar, which she animated and whose movements she defined. She seemed to be in a state of flow that Caspa didn't dare to interrupt. Her brush captured her real movements, and as she swayed back and forth, so did the avatar she drew on the easel. After a while, she seemed satisfied with her work and cried out when she recognized Caspa, which quickly turned into laughter. "Sorry, I just thought the final boss of my easel really came to life."

FIGURE 5.10 The game artists Panita and Sondu.

The campfire was burning high and Caspa's brain swam in a cocktail of endorphins. They had fresh fish for dinner and the two artists were very curious about the project. Panita was calm and had a keen eye for detail, while Sondu was vibrant and used every surface as a drum kit (Figure 5.10). They made quite a contrasting pair, and both were able to enrich the atmosphere of the evening in their own way. Sondu played the guitar and sang a traditional song, while Panita and Daisy were dancing to it. Caspa recognized that the animations of her avatar were inspired by this cultural dance. After a few seconds, Casper just stared at Daisy, who was moving around the fire like a panther. In the moment Caspa found the courage to stand up and join her, the song was over. Embarrassed, he sat down again, and her cheerful laughter was infectious. Caspa and his new friends stayed up until late, lying in the sand, watching the stars and combining them to form new constellations.

STEP 5.13 CREATE A MOOD BOARD

The following morning, Panita explained the next step: "As part of the game concepting, we want to visualize our ideas to improve the communication of our vision. These initial visualizations are called concept art and can be generated by an artificial intelligence, but obviously I prefer having it done by a game artist. The game artists will get very active in the game construction phase, creating all visual and sound assets to shape the game experience. However, having early sketches of characters, the environment, and also the potential camera angle will help us to bring the mental vision of the game to life. The created concept art can be supported by inspirations from existing games, and also from other media like movies or historical photography. The corresponding artwork is collected on a so-called mood board as a reference for the entire team. You can have several mood boards with different art approaches and gather feedback from the team, commissioner and the target group which art style would best serve the game.

Be aware that the selection of art can also support the delivery of the subject matter. If you have a historical game, you could create the entire art style inspired by the corresponding art era. A game about depression could have an inner, dark atmosphere that is in contrast with the bright exterior. Even if it's just labelled as an initial approach, concept art heavily influences the vision of the game for the team and especially the commissioner, so make sure to get their feedback and agreement. Especially for people not working in the gaming industry, a picture is much more tangible and intuitively understandable than the description of the game mechanics."

Sondu added: "I will select an initial soundtrack for the game to support the communication of the atmosphere. Later in the process, I might compose and record an own soundtrack along with further sounds, but for now I will just buy one from an online library."

STEP 5.14 SELECT THE MOST PROMISING IDEA

After another day, Caspa and Daisy had ten different game ideas, each of them enriched by initial concept art.

"Sooner or later, we need to stop the massive idea generation process and go for the most promising approach. In idea selection, we need to combine, merge, adapt, kick out and sometimes even create new ideas. It is one of the hardest things to do in the entire development process, and one of the most important decisions since it will have a massive influence on the final shape of the serious game. In theory, we can always jump back to the prior phase or try out a totally different approach, which we should do if our first shot isn't working out. In practice, however, 80% of the projects are sticking to this first selection, defining the shape of the game. In the idea selection step, it is more important than ever that individuals are able to kill their darlings, the ideas that they personally like most. Even if intuition still plays a role, we should base our decision on objective criteria. You can use an idea funnel and add certain requirements to it.

If the idea goes through the funnel, it goes to the next round, in which you can apply a finer mesh sieve. Some criteria that we used in the past:

Is the idea...

- ...desired by the target group?
- ...able to achieve the project goals?
- ...synergize with the subject matter?
- ...having a promising coreplay that supports the subject matter?
- ...doable given the project limitations?
- ...efficiently realizable according to the skills of our team?
- ...inclusive and ethically appropriate?
- ...up-scalable and sustainable?

Of course, you can add further criteria to the funnel and adapt it to the project. Having the analysis report and impact intension at hand will help you to keep an overview. At the end, you will end up with a handful of ideas that made it through the selection. See if you can adapt and merge them into a single shining star. If not, keep the best three to five idea candidates and present it to your commissioner or the target group.

At the end of the process, you can also work on several candidates in parallel and let them evolve, which is just a possibility if you have the necessary time, resources or several teams that can work on the candidates at the same time. After a short period, you can go for the grand finale and select the most promising one, or again merge them. I highly recommend not waiting for too long and focus on one as soon as possible. Your resources and time will run out sooner than you think, and having all your teams focus on one candidate early on will increase your chances of realizing a successful project."

While following the process, Caspa knew that he would never again meet a person like Daisy. He was fascinated by her way of thinking. Her two-coloured eyes represented the symbiosis of fun and seriousness, her creativity was inspired by the beauty and heterogeneity of nature and cultures from all over the world. Caspa didn't see a ring on Daisy's finger, but he was too afraid to ask if she was married.

Derren supported digitally. By using the idea funnel, he narrowed their ideas down to four (Figure 5.11). It was about time to get feedback from the target group and the commissioner, and therefore, Caspa had to arrange

FIGURE 5.11 The idea funnel as a selection tool.

his travel to the academy. He couldn't believe his ears when Daisy said she would follow in a couple of days and support him further.

STEP 5.15 BUILD MANY PROTOTYPES

Back in the academy, Caspa worked hard on the game candidates, showed it to the target group and updated the analysis report on a frequent basis. Based on the feedback of the target group and the commissioner, Derren eliminated another game candidate straight ahead, which was a pity because it was Caspa's favourite. Actually, Caspa didn't like Derren's harsh procedure. It seemed that he didn't recognize the amount of effort Daisy and Casper invested in these ideas! Prombu digitally pushed Casper to continue on the process, and he felt additional pressure on him. It was time to build some prototypes.

Daisy explained: "Prototyping is a task that we are doing very often along the process, and now it is a good time to bring the candidates to life. No matter how complex your game might be at the end, you can always build a low-resolution prototype to test a certain aspect of the system.

This is also a good time to speak about the user interface (UI), defining what is visible to the player and how they can navigate through the game. You should also consider the creation of wireframes that showcase the logic of your system from the user point of view (Figure 5.12). What happens when the user clicks on this button? Which screen will appear? How can they go back?

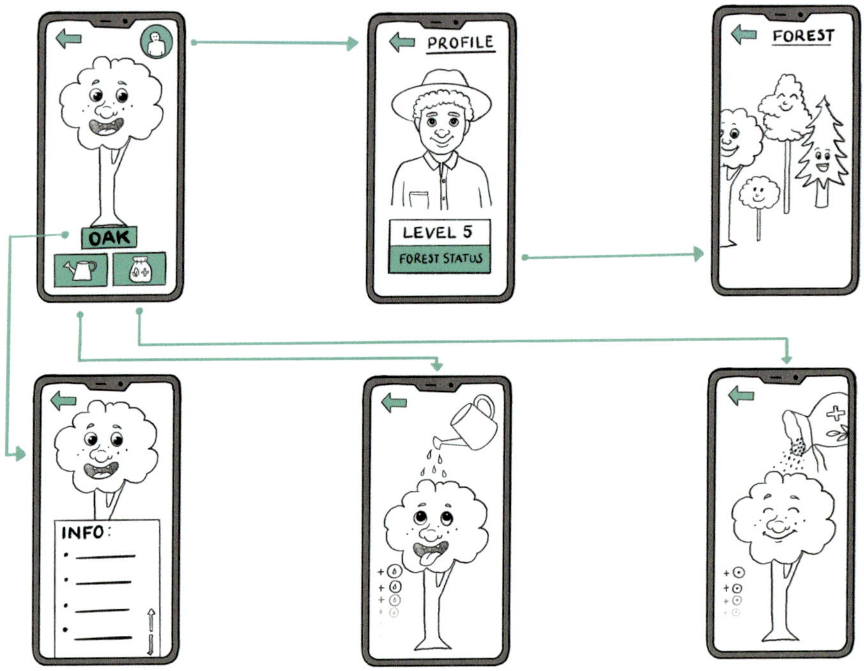

FIGURE 5.12 An example of wireframes.

You can use any analogue material to help you simulating the game experience, and the more your testing group can actually interact and test the prototype without you explaining how it works, the better you can check if your system works. Don't try to integrate the entire subject matter into your prototype, just select one aspect and see if you can incorporate it into the game experience. You can also create digital prototypes on digital whiteboards or applications made to create digital low-resolution prototypes. You can already throw in some conceptional art and sound if you like. Let your user click through the logic of your wireframes, even if it is just on paper.

Don't be afraid of presenting something that looks not much better than the outcomes of a children's birthday party craft activity. Actually, sometimes you receive more honest feedback from your testers if your prototype is not looking final, especially if they don't want to hurt your feelings. If you build the prototype by yourself, you can start playing the prototype on your own, even if you develop a multiplayer experience.

If we build the prototype as a team, we can test it internally between us and then inviting some friends to play it. Having access to the target group, we should already give it a shot in a small test round. The earlier we collect feedback the better. Always be aware that you have to be careful to handle this feedback. User feedback is super valuable to figure out what is not working with the game rather than giving you the perfect solution for it, especially if they are not trained game designer. Be aware that the testers might crush your idea.

But don't give up: If you realize that your idea is not as good as you initially thought, stay resilient and don't throw it away immediately. Iterate and improve, don't take it personal. There is probably a reason why it made its way through your idea selection. This is also a great moment to get feedback on different art styles, selection of sound but also the initial world building and story, if you already have certain options.

Make sure to note down their feedback. You can either record the feedback session, you can ask them to fill out a questionnaire with qualitative and quantitative feedback, you can interview them, but you can also just make some notes. Check about if they enjoyed playing the prototype, but also see if the subject matter was delivered."

After prototyping and testing the game candidates, Daisy and Caspa were able to identify the most promising approach, enriching it by a core idea of another candidate and finally, it was in front of them. A chaotic mix of papers and tangible objects, a low-resolution prototype representing the entire game experience.

"Isn't it beautiful?" Daisy smiled at their baby. "This is playable 1 (P1). Now it's time to fill it with bones."

STEP 5.16 DEFINE GAME DESIGN PILLARS

"Agreeing on game design pillars is a useful way to give guidance on all design decisions of the game. They usually try to express a feeling, emotion or specific aspect of the player's experience. In most projects, we identify 3-5 game design pillars that help us to navigate through the creation process. Make sure that the commissioner is agreeing on the pillars, ideally, they were part of the decision process to increase ownership."

After brainstorming a while, Daisy and Caspa came up with the following game design pillars (Figure 5.13):

1. Inclusiveness: The game is as inclusive as possible and covers different point of views.
2. Accessibility: The game is accessible also with low-end devices and weak internet connection.
3. Decision-making: The game allows the player to make meaningful choices as often as possible.

FIGURE 5.13 Game Design Pillars.

"Wonderful. The game design pillars can be adapted throughout the conceptualization phase, but once the construction begun, we should try to avoid changing them. But for now, we are good to go."

STEP 5.17 CREATE AN IMPLEMENTATION STRATEGY DOCUMENT

Caspa had a call with Anaka to update them on the progress. They were impressed and gave further advice.

"Zoom out from time to time, even if you are in the middle of the creation stage. Sooner or later, you will hopefully have a game and then the implementation starts. You should be prepared for this. In your high concept note at the beginning of the process, you already had a rough idea how you want to implement your solution with the target group. After the analysis and having a clearer idea on the context and your solution, you should revise and update your initial implementation strategy.

Will you develop a digital game and try to get your target group onboard with paid advertising, community building and online workshops? Will it be supported by offline events and physical workshops? Will it be an analogue serious game that you have to deploy to your target audience? Gather first ideas in an implementation strategy document that will be updated along the process. We will speak about this in more detail in stage 3, and already at this point you should have a plan how you want to approach your target audience."

STEP 5.18 DESIGN IMPACT MEASUREMENT SYSTEMS

Derren and Casper booked a tiny room in the academy's data centre to discuss the next steps. Casper presented the current state of the game.

"I am impressed, the low-resolution prototype is in a good shape. To gain a better insight on the impact of our project, we can incorporate impact measurement systems (IMS) into the game. They mainly serve to provide direct qualitative and especially quantitative data, so don't forget to collect indirect data as well. This said, the IMS can't be the only tool that you use in order to evaluate your project, it is just one piece for your evaluation portfolio. Adapt your IMS to your impact intention. Here are some of the systems that I designed or used in past projects:

- Platform statistics – This data can be harvested from our platform or the stores. It is data like number of downloads, active players or the dropout rate, and can also give us information about devices or the region the player is playing from, depending on the data guidelines and settings.
- In-game data – Anything that happens in a digital game can be tracked, for instance how long you watch a video or which decision you make in the game. Make sure to track relevant actions of the player, like player performance related to subject matter, in-game interaction with other players, etc.
- In game questionnaires – Integrate a pre-, post- and longitudinal questionnaire. The pre-questionnaire is submitted before or within the first hour of playtime. The post-questionnaire is submitted after playing the main storyline of the game. The longitudinal questionnaire is submitted three months after the post-questionnaire is submitted and checks if the game had a mid-term impact on the player. Don't include too many questions. Gain information about opinions, awareness, first impressions and demographics.
- In-game experiment – Divide the players into groups and provide them with slightly different aspects within the game to check on

different in-game behaviour or variation on the subject matter performance. For instance, Group A receives in-game propaganda, Group B receives objective news and Group C receives no news. Is it resulting in significant changes how they treat in-game refugees or how they answer the post-questionnaire?

- External experiment – Include the game as one variable in a classic experiment with three different groups. For instance, define a timeframe of 6 weeks. Group A is forced to play the game for a certain amount of time, Group B has access to the game but can play on a voluntary basis and Group C has no access to the game. Check how to groups perform before and after the experiment on the subject matter.
- Real-life challenge – Kick out the player from the magic circle by requesting tasks in the real world. For instance, you could challenge a player to apply three small changes in their school to create a better learning environment and later upload three pictures witnessing their actions to the game.
- Tests and assignments – Compared to questionnaires, tests and assignments aim to measure knowledge and skills rather than awareness and opinions. You can include them very explicit as exams; however, a less disruptive experience would be an elegant integration as in-game relevant boss fights, synchronizing gameplay with subject matter.

The evaluation and player feedback, for instance through tests or real-life challenges, can be done either via artificial intelligence, other peers or players as well as dedicated moderators or subject matter experts, based on the complexity of the task and the project frame. Data privacy and security is of high importance, especially if you collect personal data. Especially in fragile contexts, data leaks of your IMS can lead to personal security risks of players.

Be aware that data can be heavily biased through wrong designed triggers and extrinsic rewards. If you announce that you will reward your player with a big amount of in-game gold if they answer a few questions, they might not take the questions seriously and quickly click through it to get to the reward. From my experience, kindly asking them for honest feedback to improve the serious game leads to less data but more meaningful feedback.

Another tip is the tracking of the response latency. If every question is answered within less than a second, the likelihood is very high that the user just skip-clicked through the questions to get to the end. Collect all answers, but tag data has a different response latency than 2-15 seconds. Of course, adapt the accepted response latency based on complexity of questions or the use case.

STEP 5.19 CREATE A GAME TREATMENT

The feedback from the target group lead to an adjusted game candidate, which was evolving with the game design pillars. Through the implementation strategy document, we have a rough idea how we want to implement the game. This project progression based on feedback by the target group will give the game treatment much more credibility, since we gathered some early proof that the game approach is fun and effective.

The game treatment is a document that is more elaborated than the high concept note, describing the genre, setting, narrative, characters, game loops, etc. in more detail. It is supported by concept art to visualize the atmosphere and gameplay experience of the game. Next to the potentially updated impact intention, the serious game treatment should include a summary of the analysis phase, putting a special focus on the target group and the context. You should also have a first idea on the technical construction of the game, on what devices it will be available and what kind of requirements are needed to play the game.

An important section is the overview of the learning content or subject matter and how it is integrated into the game experience. Next, the game treatment should give an overview about the impact measurement systems, how data is generated, collected, secured and evaluated. There should be a section that describes the strategy of accessibility, upscaling and sustainability as well as a section how game ethics and an inclusive approach will be realized. Finally, you can add an initial promotion and implementation strategy.

A game treatment of our game could be structured like this:

- Cover, consisting of an appealing illustration, the name of the game and the name of the team.
- Problem statement, combined with a personal story that the reader can relate to.
- The solution, game approach, genre, setting, subject matter and targeted platforms.
- Product in action, a concrete visualization of the final experience. It can be supported by pictures from early-stage testing.

- Impact Intention with operational key performance indicators.
- Market and target group, ideally with demographics and iterated number of potential users.
- Existing solutions, competition and why the game is of added value.
- Summary of the outcomes of the analysis phase.
- Core team, including roles and main responsibilities.
- Process map, timeline, including different phases and milestones.
- Updated financials, including estimated costs and exit points for the commissioner.
- Details on the selected subject matter.
- Game ethics and inclusive approach.
- Game narrative, environment, characters and story progression.
- Gameplay in combination with subject matter and game design pillars.
- Game atmosphere and intended emotions of players.
- Mood board and concept art.
- Impact measurement systems and data security.
- Technical implications, information on required devices, etc.
- Accessibility, scalability and sustainability.
- Initial implementation strategy.
- Call to action, requests, funding for the next phase and further information on the project context.
- Contact information.

Some aspects might require more than one slide, but try to keep the game treatment sharp and lean. Next to being a great summary of the work so far, it is often used to raise funds and convince the commissioner to finance the next phases of the development process. It should incorporate high-quality visuals, and you can also add explanatory videos for key slides and make use of a potential initial soundtrack, supporting the communication of the game's atmosphere."

STEP 5.20 REACT TO A CHANGE OF REQUIREMENTS

Spending time at the academy together, Derren, Daisy and Caspa finalized the game treatment and presented it to the commissioner. Caspa feared that their shared time would end soon. The meeting took place in the office of the professor and Prombu joined digitally. Even though Prof. Monty had many detailed questions in the meeting, he was pleased with the quality of the document and the corresponding prototype.

"You did a good job. However, I want you to add a digital serious game version. It should connect all students from the academy, not only the ones that are sitting in the same room. You also have my confirmation that I will fund the next phases of the project."

Caspa was still stunned from this meeting. The commissioner changed the initial requirements which caused substantial changes in the game design and also in the entire game development process. Did the professor do this on purpose? Prombu and Derren had a heated argument after the meeting. Such a late change in requirements is usually not manageable, and Prombu knew Monty was aware of this (Figure 5.14). Was he toying with the team? Caspa suspected that the professor had some aversion against Prombu. Was he jealous of her success? Or did something happen while they designed the crisis simulation of 2040?

FIGURE 5.14 Clash of team members.

Derren seemed to have agreed to the changes too quickly, and Prombu was about to pull out of the project. Casper didn't get the details because he and Daisy gave them some privacy.

Casper sighed. He would require support by additional people to realize a digital version.

STEP 5.21 SET UP THE GAME DESIGN DOCUMENT

Daisy, Derren and Caspa sat together in the flourishing green belt of the academy. It was situated around a hill, and the three game developers had a beautiful view of the tiny village, which nestled picturesquely in the nearby valley. They saw quite a big construction site in which humans and robots were collaboratively paving the ground for a new building, probably the new elementary school that was planned some time ago. Daisy supported Caspa doing additional analysis and adjusting the prototype according to the change of requirements. Caspa was tired and had dark circles under his eyes caused by late-night working sessions.

He would have loved to have the picknick with Daisy alone, and he felt honoured and was equally annoyed once Derren invited himself to support. Caspa sensed that there was something going on between the creative director and Daisy, even though he was married to Prombu. Derren looked at the updated game treatment that Caspa was working on the last days.

"I really like the changes that you made according to the new requirements from the commissioner. My intuition tells me that we are following the right approach. We will further conceptualize, prototype and test the approach for sure. But I believe we can already start to set up the structure of…"

"… the game design document!" Caspa didn't like the way Daisy finished Derren's sentence, nor the smile they shared afterwards. He tried to pull himself together.

"Isn't it a bit early for the game design document?"

"The game design document, or in short GDD, is a living artefact. The document is updated and receives new content on a frequent basis until the end of the project. Even though it is a living document, it is also a central milestone in the development of serious games. Game designers, programmers and artists can use it as a blueprint and reference and therefore forms the basis of the construction phase. The GDD must evolve with the process along the way. Because it is a central point of reference, it needs to be clean and tidy at all times. The game director is responsible for the overall management of the GDD; however, other team members can also make changes. Progress on gameplay, narrative, atmosphere, subject matter and impact measurement systems is recorded centrally in this document. Even though the GDD is constantly evolving and growing, it should reach a certain level of maturity before the programmers can begin their work. This will help the producer to keep an overview about the timelines.

The idea and logic of the game should be clearly recognizable, and also by people who are not yet familiar with the game. The construction has not yet begun, which is why changes can be made quickly and cost-effectively. I try to reach a maturity of roughly 60–70% completion before giving the GDD to the commissioner or other relevant stakeholder for feedback. We can expect a lot of suggestions for changes in this step of the process, so aiming for 100% completion in the first shot would be inefficient."

"How does a GDD look like?"

"In some projects, it is just a text document with some tables. In others, the GDD will be split up into different components, and the sum of the components form the GDD. Depending on the game, you could have a world design component, a narrative and dialogue component, a character design component, a map and levels document, a rulebook, a balance sheet, a style guide, a flow board etc. It also contains the minimum viable product (MVP) definition, which describes the absolute minimum requirements of the game to be realized to be able to achieve the project goals, but we will get to this later in more detail. Sometimes the GDD is more like a shared folder consisting of different subfolders for each of the relevant subcategories of the game (Figure 5.15). Hence the content of the folders needs careful curation by all editors. As you can see, it is a colourful bouquet of many different elements that describe the game in its entirety as detailed as possible."

Daisy pointed to the construction site in the valley. "The builders down there also had a plan done by the architect before they started the construction of the house."

Caspa laughed heavily, a little too loudly for it to appear natural.

FIGURE 5.15 The simplified folder structure of a game design document.

STEP 5.22 CONSIDER DARWINIAN GAME DESIGN

It was not easy to spend time with Daisy in public, since most students recognized her and wanted to take some pictures with her. Furthermore, Derren was strolling around the campus, and Caspa hated himself for not appreciating the support he received from him. After a clarifying meeting with Prombu, she agreed to further support Caspa and the project. But she seemed seriously annoyed by the professor.

The analysis report and the GDD was updated on a daily basis, while the subject matter list stayed more or less the same. Derren gave insights on some game design techniques, and Caspa tried to incorporate as much as possible into the game.

"Under Darwinian game design, I understand a mindset that attempts to learn from evolution. Follow me on this mind game, cutting out the comforts of civilization. As infants, we need the security of our family to survive. We might feel the urge of competing against our siblings to receive love of our parents, searching for affection and care.

As we grow up, we must learn what it means to become an adult and seek the acceptance of a group. We form a broad-based clan consisting of specialized individuals that contribute to the clan to increase our likelihood of survival. We must find our place in this clan, specialize and learn to become better in our role, performing in an energy-efficient manner. We possess an intrinsic motivation for learning to improve ourselves and satisfy curiosity, and we also learn to get a better reputation and increase our status to be valued by the clan.

When we build a family, we take care of our children and protect it with our lives. When we grow old, we share the wisdom with the entire clan by storytelling so our kids and grandchildren have a better chance of surviving and our DNA outlasts. This mind game is a heavy simplification, and still can help us to identify and explain very basic human interaction patterns that were valid for the last two million years. Think of modern traits like status or fame. This desire for admiration is based on group acceptance and dictates modern societies. Think of other examples of modern behaviour and see if you can't trace it back to survival strategies of our ancestors (Figure 5.16).

What can we learn from it for our games?

FIGURE 5.16 Darwinian game design.

This Darwinian thinking will help you to identify whether a mechanic or artistic approach is following the patterns of basic behaviour that helped our ancestors to survive. The fundamentals of visual art make use of this all the time, for instance a final boss consisting of pointed triangles that subconsciously remind us of thorns, teeth and danger. Role-playing games gather a team of different specialists who form a functioning group that can survive in the environments by supporting each other. Fulfilling this primal need for social interaction in games can be highly rewarding for players, so be sure to consider it in your game design.

STEP 5.23 CONSIDER THE EVOLUTION OF YOUR USER

The following model is inspired by the flow theory, the Octalysis framework[4] and visualizes the evolution of the player. While a player is going through the different user journey phases, you should adapt your design accordingly. Extrinsic motivators are a great way to give a quick overview on how to behave in a system, and bit by bit they should be accompanied and replaced by intrinsic motivators. Let's check out the different phases of a user journey of a serious game (Figure 5.17).

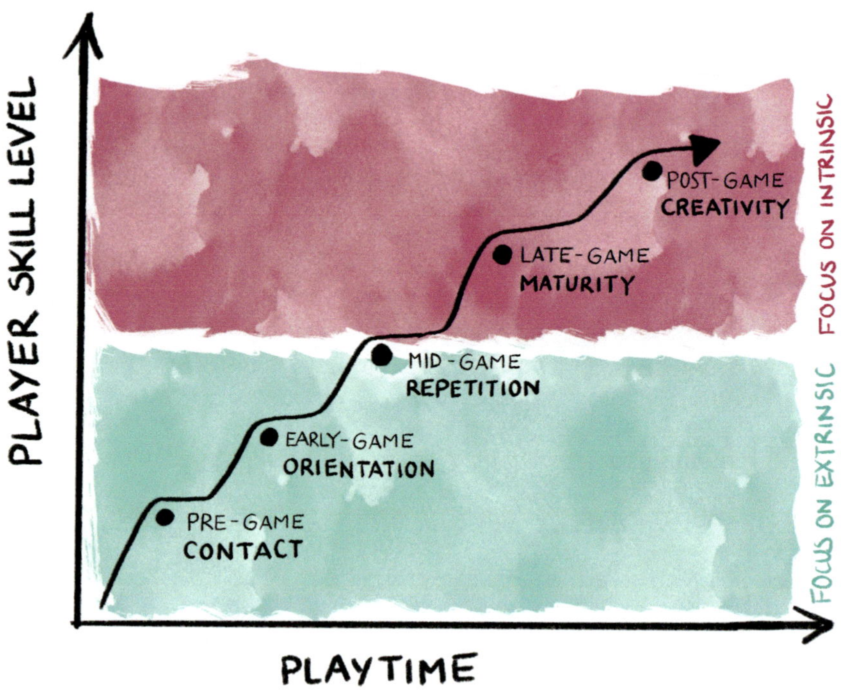

FIGURE 5.17 The evolving player.

- Pre-Game: This phase is determined by the first contact the target group has with the project or game before they play it. For example, through advertising, a recommendation from a friend or approaching our stand at a conference. This first contact already shapes the user's expectations of the game and therefore has a direct influence on the gaming experience in the player's mind once they actually play the game.
- Early-Game: When the player plays the game for the first time, the player needs a well-designed first-time user experience (FTUE). The player should understand why the game is relevant and fun and get some first moments of success. Don't make the mistake to make it too easy, hook the player through challenges. Extrinsic motivators will help to provide an overview and orientate in the system.
- Mid-Game: After playing the game for a while, the user should experience progress and follow the path to mastery. The core game loops repeat, and the player is getting better each time performing it. The mid-game is a good way for increased interaction with potential other players and to unlock new features while the coreplay stays the same.
- Late-Game: The player is approaching mastery and is aware of all the functions of the game. Extrinsic motivators such as status are still working elements, and intrinsic motivators are becoming increasingly important. Becoming a game mentor and guiding new players, unlocking and beating the hardest difficulty levels can define the actions of these mature players. In serious games, the mature player is close to mastering the entire subject matter.
- Post-Game: When designing this phase, try to unleash the creativity of your players. They mastered the game and know it by heart, and it would be a pity missing the opportunity to let these hardcore fans build on it. Map creators or Blanco cards can encourage them to create own content and share it with the community. Consider the build of mods or modifications, allowing users to reuse the skeleton of the game and transfer it to a new setting, for instance. Let them add additional subject matter and think about an approval system. Just a few percent of your players will reach the post-game phase, but they can become powerful multipliers and should be appreciated and supported accordingly.

Derren smiled: "Game design is a craft, and let us continue by learning from a person who mastered this craft. Evali, please play the Mind Games Blink by the inspiring Jake Manion!"

GUEST BLINK JAKE MANION, KENYA: CONTEXTUALIZED GAME DESIGN

Jake Manion has been working in video games for over two decades now as a producer and director, and is going to share a bit on his approach to designing for serious games. Much of his time has been spent working with organizations like public service broadcasters and international development agencies, who use games as a means of communication with their intended audience. Several projects Jake worked on have attracted recognition like Children's BAFTA nominations, and one game even won TIGA's "Best Game with a Purpose" the year it shipped. Jake is British and was based in the UK until 2016, and since then he has been doing this work from Kenya, often with a focus on players across Africa.

Understanding Your Subject Matter

Most game productions are incredibly complex beasts that need to be managed from lots of different angles; technically, emotionally, artistically, commercially and many more. A Serious Game introduces an additional angle – the overall objective of the product, be that helping European kids understand the subtle complexities of sustainability or teaching best practices for rural smallholder farmers in Kenya. Whatever that objective might be for your production, it's unlikely you're enough of an expert yourself.

So for me these projects always start with a huge amount of research into the subject matter; working with experts throughout the entire process, trying to understand the subject inside out, looking at traditional methods of delivering the message (you don't always have to reinvent the wheel) and exploring existing media – especially any games – that have already attempted it. I've had the privilege of working directly with several of the most preeminent scientists in their fields, and it's a very special experience to have the access and time to learn from them and translate their expertise into game designs.

As a designer or product manager, you can see yourself as the conduit between the player and your product's objective, and so any misunderstandings you have will be passed on to the player, which could seriously affect how well the game meets that objective.

Designing for Subject Matter

Now, with all that said, it's also really important that you don't unwittingly allow all that fascinating information to completely ruin your game. There are good examples of successful titles in the space where had the designers tried to cram in all the details, realities and complexities of their subject matter, their games would be too overwhelming for anyone to enjoy.

I've certainly fallen victim to that myself. It's up to you as a designer to gatekeep the content and abstract it so that the relevant stuff gets through without it damaging the enjoyability of the game.

So what are some methods for getting subject matter across through an enjoyable game? First off is to get to know your genre. With all the subject matter understanding stored safely in the back of your head, go ahead and spend some significant time playing comparable commercial games. What makes them enjoyable? How could each aspect of the experience be adjusted to support your product's objective? Don't be afraid to stand on the shoulders of those giants. And when you're working in a specific genre or genre mix, understand what player expectations are from it, and only deviate from that familiarity when it genuinely adds to the experience. Players will likely have enough to think about without learning new paradigms.

Once you've really gotten to know your genre, you can think about how best to weave your subject matter through the gameplay. You could do it through linear and non-linear storytelling – using your narrative, characters and world building to communicate a meaningful story. You could use clever gameplay mechanics to reinforce the player behaviours you're trying to communicate – rewarding desired behaviours, and even punishing the opposite, to gradually reinforce your game's message. You could even go all out and use your game to realistically simulate your subject matter. A good simulation is a safe environment where players can experiment with behaviours and their consequences, though often you'll come up against a tricky trade-off between realism and enjoyability. In practice of course it's likely you'll opt for a mix of these approaches.

Seeking Feedback

The process of getting all this design stuff right for your players starts with research and that mindset should continue throughout your development process. This takes the form of ongoing testing – by yourself, with your team and most importantly with your intended players.

For example, you could present early experiments in visual identity, character designs or narrative to a small group of players, and informally see what they think. Ask what they like, what they're feeling and why. With an early gameplay build, you can be observing them to ensure they understand how to play, what they're meant to do, feeling the emotions you intended and comprehending your message. And, of course, you can seek insights into whether they would actually install the game and spend enough time playing it, as all your efforts won't count for much if they don't!

You can test out each aspect of your production separately, and as a whole, at almost any stage of production … though the earlier you discover design issues the more likely you'll have the time and budget to fix them. And during these testing sessions, you should take extra care to identify and diagnose the real problems and their root causes before jumping into solutions, as trying to solve an inaccurate or non-existent problem will just waste time and make issues harder to fix later.

Cultural Research

I've worked a lot on cross-cultural games, aimed at players in quite different contexts to my own, and these often include depictions of their own lives and surroundings. This is very easy to get wrong, often due to assumptions about places, cultures or people which are based more on common stereotypes than reality. Players can often detect that kind of inauthenticity a mile away, and when they do it becomes extremely challenging to build enough trust with them to deliver your message effectively.

Overcoming this issue takes some time but isn't very hard, and yet again starts with good research. Take the time to observe and understand the place and people you're depicting, and be aware and critical of any assumptions you're making about them. This applies equally to storytelling, art, gameplay and your game's entire visual identity.

For a branding example, an educational game I once worked on in Kenya used an owl for its logo. In Europe that makes sense – owls represent wisdom. In Kenya however these birds symbolize bad omens and even death. Not great for a light-hearted learning tool for kids. Across Africa it's also still commonplace to see branding using chunky inline fonts, like that used in Jurassic Park's typography, as a lazy shortcut to communicate an "African" theme. However, this is a style from the 1920s which for decades has been widely used to represent primitive, exotic and savage places – a huge insult to any contemporary African audience.

Over and above damage control, this depth of cultural research is a rich source of new ideas and approaches, and will actually make your game much better. And achieving a considered and authentic representation of your audience might well be the first time they've ever seen themselves and their surroundings in a game – or even any media – and that can work massively to your advantage when building trust.

Conclusion

Serious Games can be incredibly rewarding products to work on. You get to become well versed in subjects you'd never normally learn about. You get to work with all manner of fascinating people with whom you'd normally never cross paths. You take on the really fun challenge of balancing all that content with some great gameplay and sit with real players to iterate until it's right. And ultimately you don't just get to entertain your players – you often get to make a real difference to their lives.

After a long call with Prombu, they agreed that it was about time to get a programming team on board. Usually, the programming team should be on board in the project framing phase, and Prombu was still upset because of the late change of requirements. Anyhow, Caspa was thrilled to meet another legend of the Mind Games Initiative: the lead programmer.

STEP 5.24 MEET THE GAME PROGRAMMER

Caspa sat in a long-distance train, a region sign welcomed him to the deep ocean region Theta. Country borders didn't longer exist, the NESGA plan divided the regions according to natural macro and micro habitats, allowing for a natural recovery process and necessary animal migration supported by humans. The programmer and her team were living in the quantum city, a place deep down in the sea to cool down the biggest server farm of the planet, a mega project from the early 40s. Corals and kelp forests were planted at the outer parts of the transparent domes, and due to the artificial light and heat produced by the underwater-city, Caspa experienced an environment bursting with biodiversity that you would usually just see closer to the surface. Even though the scenery was magnificent, Caspa had a lump in his throat and an oppressive feeling in his chest. He only felt comfortable on the water, not under it.

Most of the people living in the city were techies that monitored the calculations of the artificial intelligence NESGA. Cheng was part of the Mind Games Initiative; she and her team programmed the crisis simulation of 2040 and had the permission to stay in the city to further work on serious games for global good. Caspa met Cheng in her office that seemed like a futuristic hub, connected with server farms via massive data lines. Everything in her office was high-end technology. Even her augmented glasses were a model that Caspa didn't know existed. She had long blue coloured hair, cunning eyes and wore a stunning dress that you would usually just see in videogames, in her hand was a Rubik's Cube that she seemed to solve without even realizing it (Figure 5.18). Caspa bowed deeply.

"It is an honour to meet you, Mrs. Cheng."

After a respectful introduction, Caspa was amazed that she already promised Prombu to join. Cheng seemed to have detailed information about the entire project and explained what her tasks in the development would be.

She spoke fast and a bit unclearly for Caspa's ears: "The programmer, sometimes also called coder or developer, is responsible for the entire technical aspects of the digital game development. They bring the concept

FIGURE 5.18 The game programmer Cheng.

of the game designer to life and also integrate the art into the game code. If the game designer is the architect of the game, the programmer is the smart builder. Ideally, the programmer is already participating in the conceptualization, supporting the game designer by bringing in the technical perspective. Depending on the project, they create the digital game prototypes, iterate and improve by creating new versions of the game until it is ready to be published. The programmer is a constructor, and while creating the code they have to overcome thousands of problems that require clever solutions. Among many other tasks, they take care of the server structure, the data and database, the construction of the game itself as well as the technical implications for realizing the communication between different players or the player and the server. The programmer also needs to take care of the collected data and the security of the systems. In bigger teams, the programmers are supported by pipeline engineers that are creating own tools for the programmers, allowing them to work more efficiently. Since it still makes a difference if the game should run on PC, Smartphone, consoles, augmented or virtual reality, you need a team of developers that has experience in creating games for the chosen platforms."

It was not easy for Caspa to fully understand Cheng. Communication problems between programmers and producers or external project manager seemed to be a frequently occurring problem.

STEP 5.25 STEER THE MELTING POT

The initial idea of the game and the prototype evolved along with the team. Caspa, Derren, Daisy, Sumato, Cheng, and the artists Panita and Sondu were in frequent digital meetings to improve the initial concept. It was messy, and some tensions within the team started to raise. Caspa was overwhelmed and felt like losing control. He didn't feel empowered to handle the expectations he had on himself and called Prombu for advice.

Prombu voice was full of understanding: "No, worries you got this. Depending on the team and project, there is one step that I call the melting pot. In some projects, you have quite a polished and mature version of the GDD before the construction of the software begins. In other projects, the game programmers, artists and subject matter experts are coming in before the GDD is very mature. That is where you are right now. The team contributes with additional ideas or points at flaws in the game design, which is great. Very often, they already start to set up the project from a construction point of view and do some initial digital prototyping to test risky aspects of the game in a developer environment, checking on the feasibility of features. Artists come up with alternative assets and styles that can cause a big swing of the entire game experience. This process can easily become chaotic, which doesn't necessarily need to be a bad thing. It fosters creativity, and many great ideas and improvements are done in this step. At the same time, we have to moderate the complicated social interactions in which everybody shares their creative ideas and improvements. We want to establish a strong team working as a collaborative organism rather than having competitive individuals who are married to their own ideas and feeling personally insulted if their improvement isn't making it into the game.

From a producer point of view, this melting pot is a two-sided sword. On the one hand, the improvements can be worth the time and teams' resources. They can play around with the GDD and make it better. The team can check if the game design is totally out of scope or some features just won't be possible given the project limitations. On the other hand, many teams lose themselves in "finding the fun", getting lost in countless iterations of the game design. Having a good game director and designer will help you in the first place, but you should also set a time limit for this step if you have it in your process. As you can imagine, this is an intense phase of work for the game director as they steer the ship through choppy seas and maintain the vision. Frequent meetings and respectful communication are essential. In many teams, the code and assets that are

FIGURE 5.19 The melting pot of game creation.

developed in this step already shape the first version of the game. However, through many changes the code can get messy and therefore some teams decide to rewrite the entire code in a clean way in the construction phase. To summarize: Set a deadline to control the melting pot and take care of your team" (Figure 5.19).

STEP 5.26 DEFINE YOUR MVP

Prombu and Derren supported Caspa to moderate the end of the conceptualization phase. Certain aspects of the game were tested via multiple prototypes, and the GDD was updated on a daily basis. One day, Derren reminded Caspa that it is time to move on.

"Doing a lot of prototyping, testing and iteration, it is quite easy to get lost on what is really important for your game. Your GDD is growing and you might have had additional ideas for the narrative, new game loops, features or adaptations, and it is quite likely that all your new ideas brought the project out of its initial scope. At this point, I highly recommend to check your impact intension. Decide on what is really needed in the game and define your minimum viable product (MVP) by prioritizing the features within your GDD. The MVP is the slimmest possible version of your game. If you take out one single feature, the game wouldn't be able to achieve the project goals anymore. Defining the MVP at this stage again feels like killing your darlings, because you might really love a certain feature. But if you are totally honest, many times the game would also work without it."

"Why is the MVP definition so important? It feels like cutting out features that actually make the game outstanding!"

FIGURE 5.20 An example for a minimum viable product of a serious game.

"Of course, having all features constructed is preferrable. But you need to prioritize and be prepared for unexpectable obstacles along the way. Too often, teams invest too much time in features that are not really necessary and then don't have the time for polishing the core experience at the end. There is always more potential work than resources, and prioritization helps us to get the important things done before the resources come to an end. The MVP is formed by all features and aspects of the game that you prioritize with "must have". The items that prioritize with "should have" or "could have" will improve the game, but are not critical (Figure 5.20). We will describe the feature list more in detail, but in this step you can already write in text format what is the definition of your MVP and insert it into the GDD."

STEP 5.27 CONDUCT A DO NO HARM ASSESSMENT

The team improved the GDD and it was mature enough to submit it to the commissioner and his supporting team to conduct a do no harm assessment.

Prombu explained: "Changing the GDD is cheaper than changing the game once it is constructed. An initial GDD do no harm assessment is a great way to get feedback and decrease the probability of causing unintended harm. Especially in development cooperation, implementing games in fragile contexts or working on sensitive topics, checking on the subject matter, gameplay, narrative, art style and atmosphere is crucial to clarify whether the design is appropriate for the context and target group. This also counts for serious games in private companies, for instance if you design a game mainly in one country and then want to implement it in other offices in other countries with other cultural requirements. Since the GDD is often not a single document, the creative director should moderate through the process. We can't expect the commissioner and the team to navigate through it alone.

In one peace support game we implemented in a fragile context, the antagonist in the game wore a yellow scarf with black dots on it. When the artist created the artwork, he was not aware that a yellow scarf with black dots is a cultural artefact of a small mountain tribe, which could be taken to mean that we are making that tribe the enemy in the game, causing dangerous political consequences. These things can happen, but it is important to check and be open to adapt the assets or certain parts of the approach. The do-no-harm test is usually done in cooperation between the commissioner and a team of local experts.

NOTES

1 Braddock, K., & Dillard, J. P. (2016). Meta-analytic evidence for the persuasive effect of narratives on beliefs, attitudes, intentions, and behaviors. *Communication Monographs*, 83(4), 446–467.

2 Ryan, R. M., & Deci, E. L. (2000). Self-determination theory and the facilitation of intrinsic motivation, social development, and well-being. *American Psychologist, 55*, 68–78.

3 Hodent, C. (2017). *The Gamer's Brain: How Neuroscience and UX Can Impact Video Game Design*, CRC Press.

4 Chou, Yu-kai (2014). *Actionable Gamification - Beyond Points, Badges, and Leaderboards. Fremont.* Octalysis Media. https://yukaichou.com/gamification-examples/octalysis-complete-gamification-framework/

CHAPTER 6

Phase 6

Construction

CASPA SAT TOGETHER WITH Cheng in a meeting bubble, and they faced a fantastic view of the reef composed of numerous individual corals. A shark came by and devoured an apparently injured fish. Caspa didn't feel comfortable under the water. The last night he was plagued by nightmares of giant waves, hearing the screams of drowning people. Caspa concentrated on the GDD. They iterated on the MVP definition after the GDD went through the do no harm assessment with minor changes. It was time for the construction phase.

STEP 6.1 CREATE A CONSTRUCTION PLAN AND PRODUCT BACKLOG

Cheng had a scissor in her hand and metaphorically cut a printed version of the GDD into small pieces: "The construction plan forms the transition from the conceptualization to the construction phase. Some teams call it production plan or development plan. The construction plan takes the GDD, prioritizes its features and cuts it into parts following the divide and conquer mindset. As you know, the GDD not only describes the gameplay, mechanics, features, and the rules but also the narrative, characters and story and defines the MVP. The construction plan is more technical, trying to translate the GDD into work packages and allocates a construction time for the programmers.

DOI: 10.1201/9781003461531-9

The construction plan links work items to targets and provides a rough estimation, when the work item should be constructed. It is similar to the high-level schedule in project framing, and specialized in construction.

Target	Epic	Feature	Priority	GDD	Week 6	Week 7	Week 8	Week 9
T1	Player Progress System	XP level-up system	Must have	Page 18	X			
T1	Player Progress System	Player skill tree	Must have	Page 19	X	X	X	X
T1	Peer-to-peer communication	In-game chat	Could have	Page 48				X

This is a simplified version of a construction plan, and even this level of complexity can serve as a reference for your team and the commissioner. Nonetheless, let's go a bit more into detail and explore the different items and their hierarchy level.

Hierarchy of work items:

- Epic: A high-level structure that consists of a variety of related features. An epic could include a peer-to-peer interaction system in the serious game or incorporate a complex customizable character progress system.
- Feature: A functionality of the game that is linked to one or several epics. An example would be unlocking new skills in the character progress system by spending experience points. Another one would be an in-game chat function for the peer-to-peer interaction system.
- User Story: Usually, a feature consists of a set of user stories. The interesting aspect of the user story is that it formulates the item from the perspective of the user, often structured as "As a user from target group X, I want to share my progress in the chat, so I get recognition by other players." Playing around with user stories is especially interesting in serious games, since it gives you a sense of the underlying players motivation and whether it is aligned with your impact intention. User stories and features are overlapping many times, somehow describing a work item from different perspectives. In some projects, I don't have user stories as an own hierarchy level, but embed them in the feature description to add the point of view from the user. Try it out and see which option works best for you.

- Task: A concrete work item that the team needs to do in order to make a user story or feature come to life. A programmer needs to do certain tasks to realize a chat function in the game, for instance embedding the chat window into the user interface and also handling the interaction with the server.
- Sub-task: A task sometimes needs to be divided into certain sub-tasks. To create a sound effect of a vivid forest, you might need to record the wind blowing through leaves or buying a sound of a woodpecker from a sound library.

Don't overcomplicate things artificially if the project doesn't require it, so check with the team which structure is of added value. If you want to start easy, create a construction plan that consists of epics, features, tasks and align the epics to your targets. You can use the MoSCoW[1] principle, prioritizing items into "must haves, should haves, could haves and won't haves." You can also just distinguish between "must have" and "nice to have," whatever works best for you.

A common pitfall is the inconsistency between GDD and construction plan, since both are living documents facing many changes along the process. Some teams solve this problem by dropping the GDD as an outdated reference after translating it into a construction plan so all changes are done in the construction plan. This works for smaller projects, but the risk is that you get lost in technical work items and miss the bigger picture. Therefore, a better option is to keep the GDD updated as a major reference and link every feature to the corresponding page in the GDD.

The construction plan itself is a great tool for the producer, director and lead programmer for an overall planning and keeping track of the time. However, your team might require a list that is a bit more detailed."

"You are referring to the product backlog, right? What is the difference between the construction plan and a product backlog?"

"The product backlog is a sorted list of all features that we want to implement, including corresponding tasks and sub-tasks that are required to realize the feature. Sometimes, tasks need to be done that can be linked directly not only to a feature but also to an epic. That's fine, just mark it accordingly. The tool is meant to structure your work sprints and to help you to not invest time and optimize items that ultimately will not serve your targets (Figure 6.1). It is a further breakdown of the construction plan. Try to avoid inconsistencies between the construction plan and the

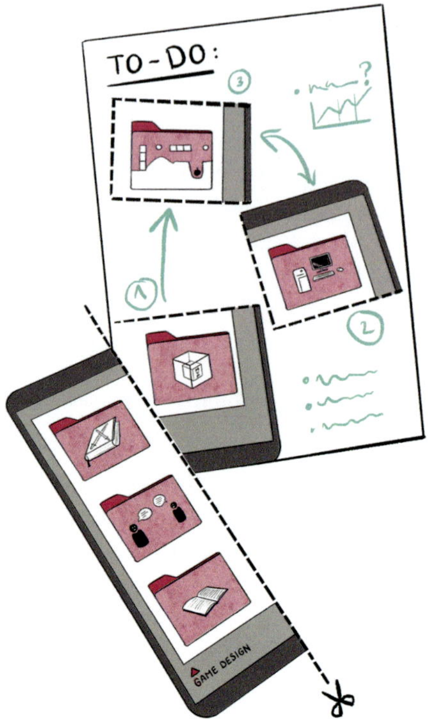

FIGURE 6.1 Transforming the GDD into the backlog.

product backlog by using a tool that allows to merge them or curate them carefully if you decide to go for two different lists. This is usually the job of the game director.

Feature	Responsible	Priority	Complexity	Tasks	Sub-tasks	Sprint	Status
In-game chat	Cheng	Could have	Medium	Realize Chat Emojis	Import Emojis	Sprint 6	In review

Caspa saw the GDD snippets in front of him. "I know we can't go into the details of programming here, but can you give me a short overview of what a programmer is actually doing?"

Cheng turned to her robot homunculus: "Let's switch the perspective and learn from a great programmer. Tron60, please play the Mind Games Blink by the fabulous Tim Hoffmann."

GUEST BLINK TIM HOFFMANN, GERMANY: TECH FOR PROGRAMMING VIDEO GAMES

After graduating in game design, game programming and -producing, Tim Hoffmann has been working on larger "Triple-A" and "Triple-I" video game projects. His role is called Build & Release-, DevOps-, or Tools & Pipeline Engineer, depending on who you ask at which company.

Only a few people outside of larger organizations might have heard about these job titles. This has at least been the case for me up until short before I have been offered my first position. It is a support role that typically does not touch anything that ends up in the game directly. Instead, the role is responsible for the process and the technological "pipeline," for putting all the pieces together to form a single product.

Imagine a semi-automated car assembly line. While other disciplines are responsible for designing, creating, and assembling the individual parts of the car (or game, respectively), my team and I are building, and maintaining, tools and the assembly line itself (in software). In theory, the better the tools and the assembly line, the better everybody else can do their work on the individual parts.

Therefore, I am not an expert in any of the individual disciplines, but I do have a solid high-level understanding of technologies utilized in making video games, especially those used by programmers and other technical people.

The key technology, at the heart of pretty much any advanced video game, is the game engine. Like a car engine, it is the piece that sets everything else in motion. Without it, you might have a lot of individual pieces of a game, and they are not doing anything.

In the context of video games, the engine is responsible for many essential things. Most prominently, for handling the game loop, it is the "heartbeat" of the game. A repeating sequence, that, while the game is running, consistently takes care of things that the game needs, usually one after the other. Some common examples are checking for user input, calculating time, processing game logic, handling network communication, calculating physics, drawing visuals on screen or playing sounds. Each example can be a field on its own, with its own specialists. And there are more things that a game engine can do.

Each execution of the game loop should roughly be happening at least 30 times per second. If a single iteration takes too long, players will notice it, for example, as undesired stuttering, or a delay between input and the expected action taking place on screen. Like how the illusion of a moving picture is created by displaying 24, or more, individual images per second. Each iteration entails a huge number of individual calculations. Therefore, achieving the desired speed of execution is a trade-off between the calculations needed and the resources available. The more capable engineers are with utilizing these resources efficiently, the more fidelity can be computed with the resources given.

It can be difficult to draw a clear line between the engine and the game itself. In terms of software, the combination of both form what the video game is. Because, fundamentally, a video game is like any other software program. It is a program that is made for the purpose of playing a specific game.

You can think of the engine as the part of a game that could be reused for other games. Most games will need functionality, that handles user input, calculates game logic, draws things on screen, etc. Engines used to be completely proprietary software, developed from the ground up, as part of a specific game. While this can still be the case today, if a game has very specific needs, most games will make use of an existing engine, that has been created as a standalone product. Some larger companies develop their own proprietary engines, but this is a costly endeavour. Creating the engine is only the beginning. It also requires long-term maintenance. Therefore, many studios choose to use existing engines developed by, and licensed from, third parties.

Examples of popular engines available to the public are, at the time of writing, Unreal Engine, Unity, Godot, Cocos2d, GameMaker Studio or Phaser.

While the engine is the most essential technological part of the game, probably the most essential tool of any developer is a text editor. Programmers write code that constitutes the program logic or even the engine itself, in human-readable text files. Since writing program code is different from writing natural language, most people prefer specialized text editors for this purpose. These, so-called Integrated Development Environments (IDEs) offer a lot of additional functionality, for example, for easily running the code as a program, or for navigating, inspecting and modifying logic that is spread across large collections of files. They can also assist the programmer in identifying errors as the code is being written, similar to spell checking in a word processor, or they might offer auto completion functionality, which helps in writing code more efficiently.

Common IDEs are Visual Studio, Visual Studio Code, Rider, IntelliJ or Xcode.

All these text files that programmers are working with add up and form a code base, that grows with time, project scope and team size. Next to them, you have all the assets and additional files that belong to the game. Think about all the visual elements, audio, animations, etc. Most of these will live in dedicated files and form a collection of game project files that can grow massive in size.

Working on such a collection of files with many people comes with some major challenges. First, you need a place where everything can live. Second, you want to avoid losing it or parts of it and, ideally, have the ability to restore older versions. Third, you need to support many people working with it. For example, you need to handle conflicts that might arise when more than one person modifies a file (if two people change the same line of code, which of the two changes is correct, or is it a combination of the two?). In other cases, you might want to separate work of developers. For example, to allow "Team A" stabilizing a release version of the game, that is soon to be handed out to players, while "Team B" can continue working on experimental features, that might break the game. In parallel, without getting in each other's way.

A very small project might get by with utilizing a simple, universal, cloud file storage. It handles the first two requirements fairly well, but it does not scale for the complexity of large teams. This is what Version Control Systems (VCS) are designed for. They come with a lot of extra functionality at the cost of added complexity. But the benefits are usually worth it, and many developers have gotten used to this kind of tool. Nowadays, even a very small project might choose to use a sophisticated VCS.

Very popular choices for game development are Perforce Helix Core or Git.

As mentioned earlier, a video game is fundamentally a piece of software. Program code is accompanied by a lot of audiovisual, and other, assets. For combining all the individual pieces, you need a build system. It is a collection of specialized software that takes the individual parts as inputs and turns them into something, which can be run by a machine. The output is platform-specific, and it can only be run by a specific type of machine. A Windows PC will require a different "translation" of a package, than a Linux PC or Mac. Each console manufacturer, or even console model, requires a dedicated version as well. The build system can handle all of this.

Building a very small game might only take seconds to minutes. But large Triple-A games can take many hours to build.

Typically, the build system comes with the game engine, and it might be a standalone software package or a combination of the two.

Building a game, and potentially many variants of it, can be tedious and time-consuming. You might need to build different versions of the game, like the release version of team A and the experimental version of team B. Both of these teams might require different output packages for different purposes, like internal versus external testing, or for various different platforms, like PC and consoles. It adds up quickly.

To make this more efficient, the process is ideally automated with a "CICD" system. This stands for "Continuous Integration and Continuous Delivery."

Whenever any developer makes a change to any part of the game, they can submit their change to the version control system. The CICD system detects the new change and automatically builds the game with the build system. Potentially multiple times in parallel, for all the different versions that are needed. Usually, several other automated processes will be happening at this stage as well, for example removing files that are needed for the development process but should not reach players in public. Or uploading new versions of the server software of a multiplayer game to server infrastructure, be it in the cloud or on-premises.

In the end, all the different versions might automatically get deployed to PC platforms, consoles or mobile phones, ready to be played and tested.

Apart from the obvious benefits of automation, another key benefit of such a CICD system is feedback. If a change, that any developer has submitted to the Version Control System, causes the build, or part of it, to fail, they will get notified. The sooner they get feedback from the system, the sooner they can fix the problem, instead of discovering it later down the line, when it might become more difficult to fix. And because everybody follows this process, this is not only faster, and less work, compared to running it locally on the developer machine, it also provides the benefit of having been put into context with everybody else's changes. Remember that, on big projects, hundreds of developers might each submit many changes per day and all of them must be functioning together to have an enjoyable, or even working, game.

What I have mentioned here are some of the most essential tools and technologies used by engineers in video game production. All projects, that I have encountered in my career, did have these in common.

This is, however, not everything. Typically, any company, or project, makes use of additional tools to meet their specific requirements. Here are some brief examples, just to give you an idea:

Plugins might get used for extending the functionality of existing tools, for example the engine or IDEs. Like "attachable modules," they bring new functionality to an existing product.

Special analysis tools might be used for investigating files, which have already been compiled to machine formats, since these files are not in a human-readable format anymore.

To counter the complexity of interacting with the version control system, special tools might be developed to improve usability or facilitate specific workflows. These tools can also be integrated with the build system, allowing developers to easily view and interact with the results of their submitted changes.

Conclusion

The list of potential tools could be extensive, but they should be introduced with caution. It is essential to balance costs and benefits, as each tool incurs expenses, whether from commercial fees or the development and maintenance of custom solutions. Sometimes, a tool may seem necessary initially, but the goal might be achievable through alternative methods. Listening to different perspectives and thoroughly understanding the problem before reaching conclusions has proven to be an effective approach.

STEP 6.2 CONSIDER AGILE CONSTRUCTION

After the blink ended, Caspa's head was stuffed with new information. For Cheng, this was daily work, not recognizing that Caspa was on the verge of being overwhelmed.

"It is unlikely that the chosen initial approach of collaboration will fit the project perfectly from the outset. It must be frequently adapted to the needs of the team during the process. Especially when you work with a new team composition, make sure that you communicate that the chosen process is just an initial approach and discuss together with the team which structure serves you best. This leads me to the Agile Manifesto by Beck, et al.[2], outlining the basic principles of agile working. These principles include the following:

- Individuals and interactions over processes and tools.
- Working software over comprehensive documentation.
- Customer collaboration over contract negotiation.
- Responding to change over following a plan.

The items on the left-hand side at the beginning of the sentence are considered more important than the items on the right-hand side. This does not mean that the items at the right-hand side are not important. Processes and tools are extremely important for efficient project management, but not as important as individuals and their interactions. The processes and tools should serve our team and be customized to our needs, not the other way around. Teams too often spend a lot of their time operating impractical bureaucratic systems, tools and processes that don't really add value. This is also true for the entire Mind Games Doctrine, the process that we are discussing here. It is just a starting point for your conversation, and along the way you should adapt the steps to fit your needs or drop them if they just cause an extra burden on you.

The second principle says that documentation and reporting is undoubtedly important, and at the end of the project, we aim to have a working serious game rather than just reporting on the game or the process. Unfortunately, this point is often forgotten especially in serious games, when documentation and reporting on conferences consume a large part of resources that could actually be spent on the quality and implementation of the actual solution. Very often the project managers are aware of it but their hands are tied, because the reports and conferences are necessary to justify the financial resources of the past period and to acquire new funds.

Let's explore the third principle, which is about relationships that develop organically. We can try to capture every little eventuality in a contract, and in most cases serious games are too complex to draw up a document that describes all possibilities. Contracts are still necessary; but the relationship between the parties is more important and evolves during the project. If we maintain a trusting relationship and act with mutual respect and common sense, we can overcome internal and external obstacles together. This counts for the communication with the commissioner and other externals but also the team internally, especially working in a consortium consisting of different companies or sub-contractors.

The fourth principle in relation to serious games development allows us to embrace change and puts the importance of initial plans into perspective. This does not mean that we should not do project planning, but we should always be agile enough to adapt our initial plans to the new circumstances, especially given the fast-changing environment of the current world. It is this fine balance of maintaining a vision, following it with resilience, and be able to adapt the way to reach it.

STEP 6.3 CONSIDER THE USE OF SCRUM

The use of the Scrum framework is a popular way to help teams getting the work done. Let's take a look at the description from the Scrum Guide[3] by Schwaber and Sutherland (2020): "Scrum is a lightweight framework that helps people, teams and organizations generate value through adaptive solutions for complex problems."

In Scrum, there are different roles that contribute to the progress of the project. There is the scrum master, the product owner and the scrum team. Schwaber and Sutherland describe the tasks of the roles as follows:

> In a nutshell, Scrum requires a Scrum Master to foster an environment where:
>
> 1. A Product Owner orders the work for a complex problem into a Product Backlog.
> 2. The Scrum Team turns a selection of the work into an Increment of value during a Sprint.
> 3. The Scrum Team and its stakeholders inspect the results and adjust for the next Sprint.
> 4. *Repeat*

As you can see, these Scrum roles are very similar to our roles. The scrum master is similar to a game producer, the product owner is similar to the game director, and the Scrum team is similar to our development team. A sprint is a protected timebox in which actual work is done by the team. The sprint leads to the increment, the added value that the product gained through the work. It can be of added value to have additional people on board to use Scrum, for instance having a single person just taking care of the responsibilities of the scrum master, a serving leader to keep the team efficient. But for now, let's stick to our serious games development roles and see what we can learn, take-over and adapt from Scrum for our construction phase.

In most cases, the producer and director communicate the progress to the commissioner and bring feedback to the next planning round with the team. In the sprint-planning sessions, the team picks the next items from the product backlog, for instance an entire feature, tasks or sub-tasks. The selection of the tasks should be done in cooperation with the game director. The sprint-planning session is followed by a sprint, the protected timebox in which work happens that leads to progress. It is of big added value to not change the requirements of the tasks during the sprint to focus the energy of the team to get work done. During the sprint, the team synchronizes in very short daily meetings and explains which work steps they have completed since yesterday, what is next and which obstacles still need to be cleared so they can get their work done.

The sprint is followed by a sprint review, in which the team assesses the progress or increment, and checks which tasks have been completed and which may need to be revised again. Let me introduce you to the definition of done. This is a description on what needs to be realized in order to call a task or feature complete. In theory, every feature should be done 100% in order to be called complete. In practice, we often work with the sentence "good enough for now" and continue with the next task to avoid that the team gets lost in perfection. It is a balancing act of deciding if the current state of the feature is good enough, because if we are too easy on this it can backfire at a later stage. The more experienced your team is, the more likely you will find efficient definitions of done.

It is totally fine if tasks need to be revised again. This doesn't necessarily mean that the responsible person is bad at their job. Mistakes happen to everybody, and it is of high importance that the team is allowed to communicate them and not get punished inappropriately. People are no machines and there could be also personal reasons why the performance this week was lower than usual. In other weeks, the performance can be

FIGURE 6.2 Slim Scrum for serious games.

higher therefore. We also need to check if our initial planning and work estimation are appropriate. This is an essential part of the agile mindset. Once an item is "good enough for now," we update the product backlog in a sprint review meeting (Figure 6.2).

I consider the most important event within the entire Scrum framework to be the retrospective. Every month, the team takes one or two hours to reflect on the month that passed. This involves finding out as transparently as possible how the team can improve itself to perform better next month. Challenges and mistakes are addressed, opportunities for optimization are discussed and success and achievements are celebrated. A successful retrospective meeting requires trust and great communication skills from the team, especially from the moderator or scrum master. People should not be denounced and punished for mistakes here, but instead opportunities for optimization should be discussed. Of course, this doesn't mean that we have to accept all mistakes and basically do no steering, but rather finding a healthy balance to interact with humans and respond to their naturally fluctuating performance. The retrospective is trickier than it seems, as it is important to avoid giving the star of the team all credits every time, while openly criticizing those who are perhaps not quite as talented. It should be about working together as an organism, rather than individual competitors. If carried out correctly, the retrospective can have a tremendous value in terms of efficiency and team spirit."

STEP 6.4 CREATE A COMMUNITY BUILDING STRATEGY PAPER

The connection was not very stable. Caspa sat in his private underwater bubble and had an online meeting with Anaka, who seemed to be somewhere in a mountainous region while a heavy snowstorm was raging outside. Anaka had to raise their voice against the wind.

"Congratulations to the GDD! Now that the construction phase started, we should set up a marketing and community building strategy. This can be done partially already in project framing or by writing the game treatment, and now having the GDD we can define a clear shape. We can also make use of visual assets that are done in construction, so it is a good timing to intensify the reach out to the audience. As evaluation and testing, community building can be seen as a cross-cutting task that continues once started. It is a science in itself and along the way I will just give you an overview about the very basics that every member of a development team and the commissioner should be aware of. In many serious games projects, the marketing and community building is outsourced to a specialist company. If we have the expertise in the team or very limited budget, the ex-coms specialist is responsible for creating a community strategy that is aligned with our overall goals and targets. The more precisely we operationalize our marketing goals and provide them with target values or key performance indicators, the better it is. In addition to simply passing on information, we want to arouse curiosity, stimulate demand from the target group and even initiate initial interactions between the target group and the project.

We have analogue, digital and hybrid instruments at our disposal. Example of classic analogue measures would be flyers, posters, magazines and also activities at conferences or physical info sessions. Digital measures include email distribution lists, advertisements on websites, videos, activities on social media, info webinars and info sessions in networks. These examples are very basic, and you should think about how you want to attract people to your solution in a creative and ethically responsible manner."

Caspa agreed: "I will start with spreading rumours at the academy and will distribute some first visual assets in the shape of play cards with a nice narrative. I am sure this will get some attention."

"That is a good idea, but make sure that you first draft a strategy paper that serves as a reference and will make your actions more target-oriented.

Describe your actions, how they contribute to the targets and how much resources in terms of budget, time and efforts they require. The community building strategy paper also incorporates the market, competitors and list relevant information about the target group."

STEP 6.5 INTEGRATE ART

Caspa and the team were working on structuring the work properly while keeping in mind that changes along the way were unavoidable. Aiming for 100% was not feasible and "good enough for now" became a phrase often heard. Cheng and her team were ready to go. The first sprint planning took place, and seeing Daisy even digitally made Caspa's heart jump. The construction started.

While Cheng was setting up the technical environments in the first sprint, Daisy did some balancing work on the analogue version of the game. Caspa was about to have a meeting with the artists. Different things happened in parallel. To be prepared, he asked Derren how the art construction is working in this phase.

Derren gave advice: "It is an iterative process, and the artists need to be in frequent contact with the programmers as well as the subject matter expert, which is coordinated by the director. We have to do a lot of decisions for the art, and it would be good to refresh our memories by watching the Mind Games Blink by the marvellous Tamer Qarrain."

The streaming of the video began.

GUEST BLINK TAMER QARRAIN, JORDAN: FUNDAMENTALS OF ART CREATION IN SERIOUS GAMES

Tamer Qarrain wears many hats! For over two decades, he has been crafting interactive experiences, juggling the roles of a programmer, 2D cartoon illustrator, music composer, video editor, and animator at his gaming studio, BeeLabs. It's a passion that runs deep in the family – Tamer's 20-year-old son is already composing music and developing indie games himself. His journey began in a simpler era, loading games from cassettes with no fancy online features or 3D graphics. Yet, even then, the thrill of gaming sparked a fire in him. By 1990, at the age of 15, Tamer knew exactly what he wanted to do: create games!

Let's delve into the process of adding art, animation, sound and more to bring a serious game prototype to life. In the following, I explain some fundamentals of art creation. But this cross-cutting one might be the most important: Understanding your audience is crucial. Knowing their age, background and gaming preferences will guide every decision you make, from art style to mechanics.

#1 Inspiration and Artistic Direction

Before diving into the development process, we delve into the treasure chest of existing games for inspiration. Exploring different art styles, game mechanics and audio elements is akin to hunting for hidden gems. This spark of inspiration helps us decide whether a charming 2D or an immersive 3D world best suits our game's vision and resource constraints. While 2D games are known for their simplicity and charm, 3D games provide a more immersive experience with their depth and realism. The choice ultimately depends on the vision for our game and the resources at our disposal. 2D games are generally simpler and have a shorter development time, with advancements in AI tools making it easier to translate ideas into visual arts. 3D games, on the other hand, require a more extensive team with expertise in various disciplines, such as modelling, rigging, texturing and animation.

After exploring existing games for inspiration, we delve deeper into specific art styles to determine the perfect fit for our game's vision. Some examples include:

- Cartoon Style: Often associated with a sense of fun and lightheartedness, the cartoon style utilizes vibrant colours, exaggerated features and simpler visual language.
- Realistic Style: Aiming for a more lifelike experience, realistic art styles prioritize detailed textures, lighting effects and accurate character portrayals to create stunning visuals that blur the line between reality and the game world.
- Pixel Art: Evoking a sense of nostalgia and retro appeal, pixel art utilizes a limited colour palette and blocky visuals. Such games remain visually appealing and engaging.
- Isometric Style: Isometric art presents the game world from a slightly above and angled viewpoint to create a strategic depth and allow players to plan their actions carefully. Isometric art is both a distinct art style and a specific type of perspective. It is often characterized by its unique way of representing three-dimensional objects on a two-dimensional plane. An isometric perspective is visually representing three-dimensional objects in two dimensions. Unlike traditional linear perspective, where objects get smaller as they fade into the distance, isometric perspective maintains the same scale for all objects, regardless of depth. This is

achieved by aligning the axes of the object to the grid at 30-degree angles from the horizontal, creating a more uniform and consistent representation of space. There is no vanishing point!

#2 Concept Art

Once the art style is chosen, concept artists take the centre stage. They translate the director's vision into initial sketches and illustrations. These visual blueprints establish the overall aesthetic of the game, from character designs and environments to user interface elements. While the creative process is exciting, artists also face challenges. Maintaining consistency across a vast number of assets is crucial. Adherence to a style guide ensures every element seamlessly blends into the established visual language. Technical limitations also come into play. Artists need to optimize their creations for smooth performance on the target platform, ensuring the artistic vision translates effectively within the game engine's capabilities.

Concept art is used to visualize and explore different ideas and aesthetics for a game early in development. Style guides provide detailed guidelines to ensure visual consistency across all game elements, ensuring everything follows a unified style. Concept art inspires the visual direction, while style guides maintain it.

#3 Types of Camera Angles in Games

The camera angle we chose has a big impact on the game experience. The most common ones are:

- First-person: See the world through the character's eyes, for immersion and realism (First Person Shooter (FPS) games, racing games).
- Third-person: Camera follows behind the character, offering a broader view (action-adventure, platformers, RPGs).
- Top-down: Directly above the game world, good for strategy and some action RPGs.
- Isometric: Tilted top-down view creating a 3D feel (RPGs, city-building games).
- Side: Fixed view from the side of the game world, common in 2D platformers and fighting games.

#4 Mastering These Fundamentals Unlocks the Magic of Bringing 3D Characters and Worlds to Life

When considering 3D, it's crucial to ensure our models are optimized (low poly). Low poly is a polygon mesh in 3D computer graphics that has a relatively small number of polygons, so that the game runs smoothly on all mobile devices, even old ones but once you have all your 3D assets in place, the process of creating worlds and level designs would be seamless and entertaining and the opportunity to transform the game to VR or XR will surely be intriguing.

- Modelling: This is the foundation of creating 3D characters, objects and 360-degree worlds. It involves constructing the basic 3D mesh, the digital geometric shape that defines the form of the asset. Imagine building a wireframe sculpture.
- Rigging: This process involves adding a digital skeleton and control system to the model. Think of it like creating the bones and muscles that allow a puppet to move. Rigging enables animators to manipulate the model's limbs, facial expressions and other features to create realistic and engaging movements.
- Texturing: Textures define the surface properties of a 3D model, like colour, texture (roughness, smoothness) and material (wood, metal, etc.). Imagine painting a detailed picture on top of your wireframe sculpture – that's what texturing does in the 3D world.
- Animation: Breathing life into the rigged and textured model by creating movement. Animators use the controls defined by the rig to create sequences of poses and movements, essentially telling the model how to move and behave within the game world.

#5 The Power of Sound: Setting the Mood

Sound is the unsung hero of game development, setting the mood and enhancing immersion like a maestro. Imagine exploring a mystical forest, the rustle of leaves beneath your feet, the chirping of birds overhead – it's like being transported to another world! By carefully selecting background music, sound effects and voiceovers, we create a symphony of sound that captivates players and brings our game to life. Every sound, button, transition and animated object must be carefully considered to create a convincing and immersive game world.

- Soundtrack: Music elevates games by stirring emotions and building suspense. Original compositions add a unique touch, while licensed music offers a cost-effective option. Both ultimately aim to create a cohesive mood that complements the entire game experience.
- Sound Effects (SFX): Sound effects breathe life into the game world, adding a layer of detail and immersion specific to different genres. Footsteps crunching on gravel in a platformer create a sense of grounded movement, while the crackle of gunfire in a shooter adds to the intensity of combat. Beyond basic sound effects, games often utilize layered audio to create a more

dynamic experience. For example, the intensity of a battle theme might escalate as the player takes damage, or the ambient sounds of a forest might change based on the time of day within the game world.

- Interactive Audio: Sound design can also be interactive, reacting to player actions and adding another layer of engagement. Music might dynamically change based on the player's actions, becoming more urgent during a chase sequence or more subdued during exploration. Environmental sounds can also be interactive. The chirping of birds might become more distant as the player moves deeper into a cave, or the sound of footsteps might echo differently depending on the material the player is walking on.
- Voice Acting: Professional voice actors in quiet recording spaces create the most impactful performances for games. However, even home studios with soundproofing furniture can work. Technology constantly evolves, and AI voice-generation tools have become surprisingly sophisticated, offering high-quality voices in various dialects and moods. While AI voices might not yet fully replace the tone and emotional delivery of professional actors, they present a convincing option for certain serious game projects, particularly those with budget constraints.

Explanatory note: Sound effects (SFX) are specific audio cues for actions or events, like a waterfall or footsteps. Interactive audio responds dynamically to player actions or game states, like a beep when clicking a button or adaptive music during combat. While SFX can be part of interactive audio, interactive audio encompasses a broader range of real-time, adaptive sounds.

Finding the perfect sound effects can be a treasure hunt. While our libraries often hold a wealth of generic sounds for everyday situations, specific details can elevate the experience. Imagine crafting the soundscape for a bustling marketplace in Marrakesh. Pre-made effects might provide a generic crowd noise, but wouldn't it be more immersive to capture the specific calls of vendors, the rhythmic hammering of a craftsman, or the chatter in a local dialect?

The good news is that technology empowers us to be resourceful. With just your smartphone, you can record those unique sounds on location. Modern AI tools can then assist in cleaning up background noise and ensuring the audio fits seamlessly into your game's soundscape.

For voice acting, a professional approach yields the best results. Recording in a quiet room with sound-absorbing furniture minimizes unwanted echoes and reverb. This ensures crystal-clear delivery that enhances the emotional impact of dialogue and narration.

#6 Using Existing Assets vs Creating New Ones

Game engines like Unity3D and Unreal Engine provide access to a wealth of resources, including libraries and asset stores, that make it easier to incorporate (VFX) visual effects and animations into games. From explosions and dynamic water effects to particle systems for dust and smoke, these pre-made assets can be purchased, customized and integrated into the game development process. This not only saves time and effort but also allows developers to create visually stunning and immersive experiences without having to build every effect from scratch. The ability to leverage these resources is particularly valuable for smaller teams or indie developers who may not have the resources to create complex VFX in-house. By utilizing these tools, developers can focus on core gameplay mechanics while still delivering high-quality visual effects that enhance the overall gaming experience.

Conclusion

Crafting an engaging game is like boarding on a grand adventure, filled with twists, turns and plenty of surprises along the way. By understanding our audience, seeking inspiration and collaborating with talented individuals, we can create immersive experiences that captivate players and leave them craving for more. Users are always looking for something out of this world, which would excite them and give them thrill, excitement and happiness!

STEP 6.6 ITERATION AND GAME VERSIONS

The code and art construction were initiated, and Prombu and Caspa had a meeting. She revealed that she had some unresolved issues with the professor after collaborating on the crisis simulation of 2040. While Prombu was making good money in the private sector, Monty went for teaching at the academy. Prombu suspected that he might be jealous of her success.

FIGURE 6.3 The evolution of game versions.

"I have to ask for a clarifying meeting with him, but for now he ignores my messages. Anyhow, we have to keep moving. Our game goes through different stages of maturity, the game versions (Figure 6.3). Let me give you an overview about versions that we use in serious games development.

- Prototype: A general term for an early testable version of the entire experience or a testable version of a sub-system of the game. Usually, there is not one single prototype in the entire process, but a big variety of prototypes testing totally different aspects of the game in different development stages.
- Beautiful corner (BC): A BC is a polished prototype to give a glimpse of how the game could look and feel in the future. Imagine a camera that only focuses on one corner of a room. In this corner, everything is as it should be at the end of the project. The graphics are beautiful, the mechanics work and we get a taste of what the game could feel like. The rest of the room is not yet created or still completely messy. The BC is a good option for communicating our vision to external stakeholders, raising budget and allowing for a short interaction with the game. As a rule of thumb, one or two scenes are shown of the game with an experience duration of 3–5 minutes. The disadvantage is that parts of the BC have to be redone when the rest of the room is designed, which means that work may have to be done twice.
- A first playable version of the game that represents the gameplay and some art to ensure that all elements work together. There can be several versions of playables (P1, P2...) that are usually shared

with the commissioner and game testers to receive feedback in an early stage of the construction process.

- Vertical slice (VC): The vertical slice is the continuation of the BC and like a slice of cake, shows a cross-section of the entire game experience. For bigger games the playtime can be 60 minutes, for smaller developments it could be 10 minutes or less. Usually, a player can play an entire level of the game in a vertical slice, with all essential mechanics already implemented, including artwork and audio. A vertical slice is a potential exit point for commissioners and investors of bigger projects, as it allows a detailed insight on how the game will look and feel in the end. If the vertical slice is well received, usually the entire cake is financed and further levels and stories can be developed. The vertical slice is already a considerable effort for the team and should not be underestimated, because in principle they are already constructing a functioning game, even if this game only consists of one level. Therefore, a vertical slice is mainly used for large and mega serious games developments.
- Alpha and Beta Version: The alpha version describes a game that is code complete, while the beta version is content complete, including all levels and the narrative. Very often, the alpha version is tested internally, while the beta version is tested with a big external audience.
- Minimum viable product (MVP): A version with the minimum requirements and essential features included, ensuring the game has all functionalities needed for launch, even if these functionalities still need to be polished. If you would remove a single feature, the serious game wouldn't be able to achieve the targets.
- Pilot version (PV): The first version of the game ready to be launched in a pilot phase in a controlled test market, for instance a single university or a single country before it gets upscaled to a bigger context, for instance a region or the global market. The PV is at least the MVP, but normally includes additional nice to have and should have features. In a perfect world, the PV incorporates all features of the product backlog. The PV is sometimes called release candidate and iterations result in multiple builds (PV1, PV2, etc.).
- Master version (MV): The master version of the game is ready to be implemented on the entire target market. Based on the learnings from the pilot phase, the master version went through some iterations and also includes the necessary localization elements to be implemented in different countries, including the translation of the game content to different languages. The master version is sometimes called master gold or final version. As all game versions, the master can have multiple builds (MV1, MV2, etc).

STEP 6.7 PLAN FOR A CODE AND CONTENT FREEZE

Weeks passed by and the game quickly began to shape. Caspa was amazed by the initial progress. He had so many ideas for additional features to add to the product backlog.

Unfortunately, Derren put the initial joy into perspective: "At the beginning, we often see quick progress in the construction phase. This shouldn't lead us astray. The last 20% take as much time as the first 80% of the construction (Figure 6.4). Therefore, we should aim for two milestones called code and content freeze.

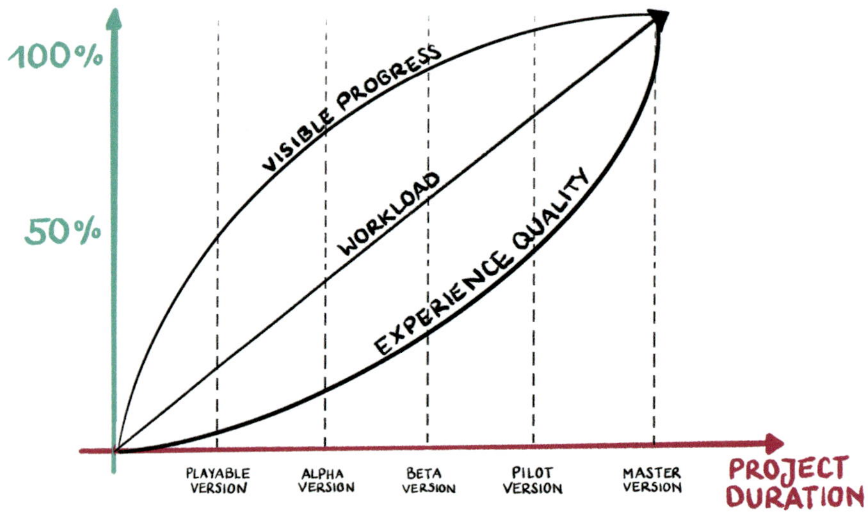

FIGURE 6.4 Game development progress.

Depending on the project's complexity, the code freeze takes place a few weeks or even months prior to the alpha version, the version that is feature complete. We tend to add more and more features to the product backlog, either because we face new requirements from the commissioner or we have new great ideas or because of the quick initial progress. A code freeze is protecting the team, especially the programmers, giving them enough time to polish and debug the game, allowing them to ship a mature alpha version.

Next to the code freeze, you can also set the milestone of the content freeze, which takes place a few weeks or months prior to the beta version. No additional content like levels, stories or subject matter should be added after this deadline, to ensure that story, levels and gameplay can be tested and improved.

Not setting a code and content freeze will definitely push the team to do overtime hours the weeks before the release of the game, the feared crunch time. Worst case scenario is that the team needs to polish and debug after the publication of the game, which can lead to a fatal first implementation and the failure of the entire project."

Caspa gulped: "Understood. Code and content freeze are mandatory. I will note down my additional ideas, but they will be parked for future versions."

NOTES

1 Miranda, Eduardo. (2021). MoSCoW Rules: A quantitative exposé (https://www.researchgate.net/publication/356836488_MoSCoW_Rules_A_quantitative_expose_Accepted_for_presentation_at_XP2022).

2 Source: https://agilemanifesto.org/

3 Schwaber and Sutherland 2020: 3 (https://scrumguides.org/docs/scrumguide/v2020/2020-Scrum-Guide-US.pdf#zoom=100).

CHAPTER 7

Phase 7

Focus Testing

THE GAME EVOLVED TO the alpha version, and Caspa was on his way back to the academy. Spending the last weeks in the underwater city with Cheng and her team of programmers was truly an experience he would never forget, but he was happy to return to the academy. Daisy was still there, lecturing on game design. How much he missed her scent!

Caspa sat in the high-speed train, petted his homunculus robot Evali and remembered the words of Prombu: "Entering the focus testing phase doesn't mean that this is the time when testing begins. Testing is an integral part of the entire process, starting with the first prototype and even with the first concept that is shown to the target group. Especially the phases construction and focus testing are heavily overlapping. Nonetheless, we should allocate a focused testing phase in which we are not adding new code or content to the game, but just polishing and debugging the game experience. It should be a strict exception that a new feature is added in this phase, even though it will be very tempting.

In serious games, the focus testing is often skipped and postponed to the time after the game is released, causing a very risky first implementation. The focused testing is there to ensure that the commissioner, investors and the target group get the game they deserve and paid for. Shipping an unpolished version will have a negative impact on your reputation that might seriously harm your business. It is way better to deliver a smaller

DOI: 10.1201/9781003461531-10

game with less features than having a big game with a lot of bugs and glitches that can't be used."

The young developer sensed that Prombu was really strict on that. It seemed to be important.

STEP 7.1 MEET THE QA OFFICER

Caspa arrived at the academy, disappointed that Daisy was on a mission with Derren. Nonetheless, he had to concentrate on the project. Prombu reminded Caspa that it was about time to find a quality assurance (QA) officer. In serious games, this role could be taken by a junior developer, but that didn't mean that it was not an important role. They agreed that Caspa could recruit a student that was about to graduate. After he posted a notice at the academy, Caspa received many applications. He went through a couple of interviews, asking the same question.

"What is your work as a quality assurance officer?"

In front of him was a young man with dark hair and large glasses, called Tesca. His toga had a small square pattern on it (Figure 7.1).

"My main responsibility is an intense testing of the game and giving feedback. This role is often overlocked, especially if the game is planning to have several testing sessions with the target group. Unlike most people of the target group, I will bring the game to its technical limits, break and exploit the mechanics to see if the balancing works and go for paths and decisions that only few players would go for. Furthermore, I will test the game on different devices and versions of operating systems which requires a good amount of time. Even if the game is fun and a great experience, the process of focused testing is not always fun. I will play the same game hundreds of times, not following the intended flow of the game, but always looking for the tiny details that could break the game. I will report all the bugs, glitches and give feedback on the design, art and subject matter in a ticketing system that I will set up and be responsible for. Finally, I will run and moderate the different testing sessions internally and with external testing groups."

It was a bit weird that Tesca carried a lot of different mobile devices with him. He seemed to have a problem with the disorder of them on the table and began to sort them while speaking. He smiled sheepishly as he recognized that Caspa watched him.

Caspa laughed: "Welcome aboard, Tesca!"

FIGURE 7.1 The QA officer Tesca.

STEP 7.2 RUN INTERNAL TESTING ROUNDS

In the days that followed, it became clear that it was not the first time for Tesca being a QA officer. He really was a lucky catch for the team, and especially Panita was amazed by his attention for detail. Caspa found that they also frequently exchanged information on a private level.

Tesca explained his system: "The internal game testing is pretty much what you would expect from a game testing process. I try to find as many technical bugs and glitches as possible and play the game with a big variety of devices and operating systems. We check on the art, animations, sound and effects and see if they are integrated properly into the game. Terrific visuals, by the way! We try to break the gameplay and the balancing, trying to find ways to exploit the dynamics and to discover superior strategies. We will play the game over and over again, and report the feedback in a ticketing system. A ticketing system can be a professional software with different categories or just a shared spreadsheet and could look like this:

ID	Build Number	Category	Name	Description	Date & Reporter	Device & Operating System	Prio	Status
71	Alpha6.1	System Bug	Load game crash	Click on load, select first game slot, game crashes	13.7. Tesca	Dreamphone 26, OpSys 5.4	Crucial	Pending

Ideally, this bug would include a screenshot or a short video to allow the programmer to track the process. You can run an internal testing round anytime when you think it would be of added value, but latest with the code freeze or alpha version, organize an explicit testing round and introduce the team to the ticketing system.

Don't underestimate how much work still needs to be done after you think the game is good to go. There is very insightful Mind Games Blink by the stunning Elisa Navarro Chinchilla, who is addressing this point among others.

Caspa turned to his homunculus, but Evali already knew what to do. The hologram video has been played.

GUEST BLINK ELISA NAVARRO CHINCHILLA, MEXICO: THOUGHTS ON ITERATION AND TESTING

Elisa Navarro Chinchilla, CEO and co-founder of Gold Bug Interactive, is a veteran educational video game developer, with more than 25 titles under her belt. Convinced of the power of games to support underprivileged contexts through collaborative learning, she has worked for NGOs and organizations such as PBS, FRP, UNODC, GIZ, McGill, amongst others.

As a serious game developer, I'd like to share four thoughts that might be useful for those considering creating games for learning. Whether you're a teacher creating a homemade game for students or developing a more professional game with a large team, these four concepts should be considered.

Thought #1: Mechanics at the Core

When considering games as a learning tool, a powerful characteristic is that in a game, you can learn by doing. We learn to walk by walking and to speak by speaking, but this is sometimes forgotten in schools where concepts are taught without actions. Games are excellent simulators for trial-and-error learning.

In a game structure, the mechanics are the actions that make the player act, like the verbs in a sentence. As Salen and Zimmerman[1] define in the book *Rules of Play*, mechanics are "the various actions, behaviours, and control mechanisms afforded to the player within a game context." Therefore, if we learn by doing and mechanics are the actions, mechanics form the core structure where learning occurs.

When designing a serious game, the first task is to determine what mechanics the game should use and what the player is learning through these specific mechanics. Many educational games neglect this aspect, resulting in "chocolate-covered broccoli" that separate learning from fun. For example, those platform games where the player is having so much fun jumping around, until they are asked a school style question that prevents them from going further. This exemplifies edutainment, where entertainment and education are thrown together as separate components. It is crucial to bind the mechanics to learning.

Thought #2: Production Decisions Affect Learning

It's crucial to have a successful conceptualization phase, with all stakeholders agreeing on the game's look, supported by drafts and visuals in a Game Design Document (GDD). If possible, gather feedback even from initial sketches.

However, the process of creating a game is dynamic. Every planned aspect becomes a decision-making exercise during development. The illustrator decides the thickness of the lines, the animator adjusts the rhythm, the UI designer adds extra shine to the buttons, etc. This creative and organic process, where collective thinking shapes the product, is key and can affect learning. If something is highlighted or unclear, or if the experience is stressful or relaxing, it all impacts the player's disposition to learn.

To mitigate this, ensure everyone understands the learning objectives. The entire team should listen to the subject matter expert and be able to explain the learning component simply. This will ensure that learning is seamlessly woven into an engaging and entertaining play experience.

Thought #3: Observation of the Player Is the Most Useful Feedback

Iterate, iterate, iterate! It is impossible to overstate the importance of iteration throughout the entire process. Continuously get feedback from your target group at every stage. Whether it's the neighbour's daughter, a local school or former students, all feedback is valuable, especially about the mechanics. Simple feedback forms or recorded interviews are useful, but observing and recording players as they play is most valuable. Note where their hands, fingers and eyes move, and where they stop. Feedback from observation can lead to new ideas, substantial improvements and crucial refinements.

Thought #4: One-Third of Development Occurs after You Think the Game Is Finished

When scheduling game production, consider the prototype, Alpha, Beta and Launch milestones. If you estimate that your game will be finished in 5 months, plan for double the time to achieve a polished and complete final game.

Conclusion

Developing serious games is a significant challenge, as it requires balancing the creation of a fun and engaging game with its effectiveness as a powerful learning tool. This insight comes from repeatedly confronting this challenge. Games from the entertainment industry have a set of well-known mechanics, so reimagining new or different mechanics for learning implies that both the game developer and the player must be open to new ways of play.

STEP 7.3 RUN EXTERNAL BETA TESTING ROUNDS

Tesca continued: "Ideally, testing rounds with the target group take place throughout the entire process and as soon as we have a prototype to share. However, once we have a beta version, we should run a specific beta testing phase. We can distinguish between closed beta phases, in which we invite certain players to join the testing experience, or we run an open beta testing phase in which basically any interested player can register for the testing.

This early access to the game can lead to valuable feedback from the players directly, but also the data that players generate while playing the game can give us insights about their in-game behaviour and if the game actually works as intended. In commercial games, especially in bigger productions with a lot of marketing and community building budget, getting enough beta testers on board is easily doable. However, in serious games, we might have the false assumption that there are endless players out there just waiting for our game and are super keen on joining the testing for free. In reality, we often face problems getting motivated players on board that are willing to share their valuable time to report on a semi-polished serious game.

Sometimes the best option is to hire and pay a testing group that is part of the target audience, especially when we have limited funds for marketing and community building. If we co-create a game with a company or a university, the target audience is more distinct and due to a closer communication, it is easier to onboard and excite them about the testing round.

Depending on the planned implementation of the game, you should adapt your beta testing accordingly. If your implementation of the final master version will be in a synchronous workshop environment, you should also organize a synchronous beta testing that is simulating this context. In these testing sessions, I like the distinction between subjective and objective data that you can collect.

Subjective data is generated by your user directly by answering questions in a questionnaire or giving feedback in an interview or in online forums. Objective data is produced by the player while playing the game, for instance checking the in-game performance of the player, measuring the players decisions in the game or using an eye-tracker tool to conduct a usability test of your game.

Some teams distinguish between behavioural data describing in-game actions or affective data describing emotions and feelings of the players. As you can see, there are limitless options how to run and evaluate a testing round, just define your procedure before running a session.

Make notes and record the overall atmosphere in the room and the interactions of the group. Are people talking about the game in the breaks, is there laughter and a good human interaction? Or are people bored, the game is not stimulating communication and people can't wait to leave the room?

It can be tricky if people with too much ownership of the game are running the testing session. They tend to defend their design decisions and try to convince players that their game is great. This can lead to a target group that is not giving honest feedback if they see that they will personally attack the moderator. That's why the QA officer is usually a good compromise, since they can say: "Be completely honest, the game is not made by me, I am just here to collect your constructive feedback."

Try to explain as little as possible. This is especially true for analogue serious games, which usually requires to read a manual before playing. The manual is part of the game, and this is your chance to test it. Everything that you explain will distort the test results.

In case you are planning an asynchronous implementation for your game, for instance if your player can play the game on their phone whenever they want or if you want to use the game as a supportive tool of an online learning course, include asynchronous testing as well to gain relevant objective data."

FIGURE 7.2 The observation of focus testing groups.

"Why is the beta testing with externals so famous? Couldn't we also run a comprehensive alpha testing cycle?"

"As mentioned, internal and external testing is something that is an integral part of the entire process and shouldn't just start by having the beta version ready. However, the beta version is close to finalization, and it will give us the possibility to test the game in a mature state, including all assets, features, levels and subject matter implemented (Figure 7.2). Try to include beta testing in every project and adapt it to the planned implementation of the game."

STEP 7.4 RUN SPECIFIC TESTING ROUNDS

Individually and in his testing rounds, Tesca found countless bugs and glitches, that were tackled by the rest of the team. Caspa thanked him for his great work, but that was not the end of testing. Tesca was on fire.

"Specific testing can be done internally or externally and will examine the game on a specific aspect, for instance on performance, accessibility, inclusion or ethics in general. A do no harm specific testing round is especially necessary in development cooperation, for instance implementing a serious game on a sensitive topic in a fragile context. Even if it is way better to receive do no harm feedback already during the conceptualization and construction phase, a final do no harm to receive green lights from the commissioner before implementation is a project requirement in many serious game developments.

Another specific testing round would be a subject matter test. We could test the game with additional subject matter experts and gather their input and feedback. Furthermore, we could run an impact test with a testing group from the target audience, examining if the subject matter is internalized by the tester and to see what we need to change to fulfil the impact intention."

Caspa summarized: "If we would have started the testing just by now, we would never be able to make necessary changes in time. Testing is part of the entire process, but the focus testing phase allows us to put the finishing touches and give the game a stress test."

STEP 7.5 INITIATE MANUFACTURING

While the digital version of the game was about to iterate towards the pilot version, Prof. Monty insisted on having a physical version of the game for the academy and added some requirements. That meant crunch time. They followed the process and conducted many testing rounds with students in a short amount of time. Daisy was invaluable working on the refinements, and also Panita did over hours to match Monty's expectations. After bringing the analogue game to a pilot version, Daisy had to go back home, working with Sondu on the sound design for the digital version. Eventually, the analogue game was ready for manufacturing.

Caspa remembered the recent guest lecture by the glorious Volker Hirsch speaking about the advantages and manufacturing process of analogue serious games.

GUEST BLINK VOLKER HIRSCH, GERMANY: THE UNIQUE SIGNIFICANCE OF PHYSICAL SERIOUS GAMES

Volker Hirsch's world changed when he was killed by a giant ant, despite his longsword, in a magical game called Dungeons & Dragons. That was over 40 years ago, and since then, he has produced all kinds of games, from children's card games to massively multiplayer online games with millions of players to serious games for professional football players.

Physical serious games hold a unique significance because they typically bring people together to play. This creates social interaction that cannot be replicated on a digital level, making such games better suited for group processes. Additionally, the tactile nature of these games engages different cognitive functions, positively impacting understanding and problem-solving. I will try to explain these aspects briefly.

Key Roles and Workflow in Board Game Development and Production

First, let's examine the basic structure of the team involved in making a board game. The author, game designer or inventor is the creative mind who comes up with the initial idea and develops a playable prototype to test with playtesters. This prototype is then pitched to a publisher. The editor at the publishing house decides if the game is viable for publishing and what changes need to be made. This stage includes illustrations, text edits of the rulebook, layout and other relevant production steps. Additionally, the publisher handles many other responsibilities such as public relations, marketing and distribution.

Once the game is finalized, it moves into the manufacturing phase, which primarily involves printing. The finished product is then transferred to a storage facility, from where it is prepared for distribution. The retailer buys the game directly from the publisher or through a wholesaler, who manages products from multiple publishers. Usually, the production of a board game or a physical game follows a standardized process aimed at reducing costs to meet a predetermined retail price point. For example, a family game should not cost more than 40 Euros in stores, allowing for a margin for the author, publisher and retailer. Consequently, manufacturing costs often need to be kept below 10 euros or less. However, with serious games, the situation is different. They are typically delivered directly to the end customer or passed through an agency without significant markup. Sometimes, the customer even manufactures the game themselves. This is an important aspect to consider in the production of physical serious games. The price of the game is usually relatively unimportant, and you should focus on producing the best possible product with maximum impact.

It may be that the usual board game manufacturers are not necessarily the best partners for manufacturing serious games. They are set up to manufacture larger print runs, starting with 500 copies for small publishers to over 100.000 copies of bestsellers. For manufacturing single or very small quantities, which is very likely for serious games, you should look for different manufacturers, such as gift-selling web shops. Very often, you will need to do the order fulfilment yourself, packing all the single pieces together into the packaging ready for your customer.

Nonetheless, I will outline a typical board game production process and then make some additional comments.

Board Game Material, Packaging and Material Sorting

Before the actual manufacturing begins, you work on the game materials you want to use. For regular board games, these are mainly paper and cardboard. Game pieces are typically made from wood or plastic, with numerous variations such as coatings or painting. For example, regular playing cards are produced with a layer of carbon to ensure that values are not visible even in extreme lighting conditions. Increasingly, sustainable materials are used, avoiding unnecessary waste to reduce environmental impact. Various certifications, such as the FSC® Chain of Custody certificate, ensure these standards.

Serious games often use less conventional materials, such as fabric for bags, magnets for games on vertical surfaces, glass marbles and more. Key questions include how often the game will be used, how many players will play it within a certain timeframe, and whether the game should be easily adjustable or modifiable in the future. Can players make these adjustments themselves?

Packaging and the sorting of materials within the packaging must also be considered. Do you need a box that can be stacked? Or a box that can hold additional material that players bring along? Maybe a bag will be a better fit? Check with your customer where and how the game will be stored. Will it be played often in a public area or used only once during an event? A good manufacturer can provide expertise in this area. Remember that heavier materials can significantly increase shipping costs.

Prototyping and Testing

In the concept phase, designers work with tools like *Excel* or *machinations.io* to ensure the concept is consistent. But it is critically necessary to build a prototype using the final materials and test it with the target audience. Very rarely are there no changes to the game rules and gaming pieces. When you test with your target audience, make sure you are not helping or influencing them in any way, as this will affect the behaviour of the players. I like the mirrored glass rooms for focus groups, where you can move to get different angles of view and discuss the situation with colleagues, stakeholders or other experts.

Once the test results show no flaws in the game rules and materials, you can start manufacturing the final product. Iteration takes time, especially if you need to involve other stakeholders. Keep this in mind when planning the milestone timing.

Selecting a Manufacturer

In the next phase, you search for one or multiple suitable manufacturers by requesting quotes after specifying your material needs. Typically, manufacturing in China is the cheapest. However, this can change if the game needs to be available quickly, making sea freight impractical. For a long time, German manufacturing was the benchmark for quality and reliability, and this is largely still the case today. In recent years, however, productions in Eastern Europe have also improved significantly. Ultimately, the decision of where to manufacture is a calculation of risk, time and cost.

Learning and Tangible Serious Games

There is plenty of scientific research on learning through experience. A great example of how this can evolve into a new approach to management processes and tools is *Lego Serious Play*. I will mention three aspects to inspire you to look deeper into the benefits of physical gaming:

1. **Motivation** – Integrating tangible materials in serious games within an educational setting involves more senses than 2D or visual experiences. These activities make learning a more dynamic and emotionally engaging process, stimulating curiosity and activating regions in the brain responsible for processing intrinsic rewards. In short: more emotions – more rewards – more motivation. You could call this "fun."
2. **Problem Solving** – Interacting with physical objects activates the motor cortex due to the manipulation of items, which is less engaged when viewing something on a screen. 2D media primarily stimulate areas related to visual and auditory processing, like the occipital and temporal lobes. Moreover, physical interaction often involves the cerebellum, which helps with coordination and precision, and the frontal cortex, which is crucial for problem-solving and planning. The richer sensory input from physical interactions helps to create more robust neural connections and memory encoding.
3. **Socializing** – While digital multiplayer environments could mitigate some of the social functions in remote work, they are very difficult to install in company settings due to security and compliance regulations. To maximize the effects of problem-solving serious games, direct face-to-face communication and cooperation are needed, allowing dialogue and conflict using all layers of communication. The game often acts as a microcosm of larger social interactions, teaching valuable social skills and strengthening teamwork.

Conclusion

Producing board games, whether traditional or serious games, is a multifaceted process requiring careful planning and execution. For serious games, the focus on durability, safety, specialized components, and educational value adds layers of complexity. By understanding and addressing these unique requirements, game makers can create impactful games that serve educational, training and therapeutic purposes effectively. Each decision in the production process, from materials to manufacturing and packaging, plays a critical role in delivering a game that meets both its functional and educational goals.

STEP 7.6 SURVIVE CRUNCH TIME

Crunching was something Caspa really wanted to avoid, but due to the additional last-minute requirements by the commissioner and some miscalculation by Caspa, the team had to enter the crunch time phase. This required the team to perform overtime hours to hit the publication deadline. The team officially can't be forced to crunch, but in reality, it was still common practice (Figure 7.3). Everybody was also intrinsically motivated to polish the game so it would be ready for the digital kick-off event with all students from the academy. The last testing rounds highlighted some issues on the game design, and Caspa used this challenge as an excuse to surprise Daisy, visiting her in her beach house. Caspa's rented travel bubble disconnected automatically from the high-speed train, and similar to red blood cells in veins the transportation system steered him from the high traffic tubes to the more remote stops. A message from Cheng popped up. She became really sick. Nothing serious, but she wouldn't be able to work at least for two weeks. Caspa was shocked. In theory, they had a backup plan, in practice, if the lead developer drops out in a crucial phase, the team has a problem.

Caspa arrived at the most remote stop of the transportation system, left his bubble and walked an hour through the rainforest to get to Daisy. The sounds of the forest somehow did annoy Caspa, he didn't perceive it as the harmonic habitat it was. He thought of it as a mess of a thousand sounds at the same time. He put on his headphones and Evali automatically played some relaxing music for him. His heart began to beat faster while reaching the beautiful beach house. In distance, he saw the door opening. Daisy opened it and Caspa felt a warm feeling in his chest. But then, this feeling

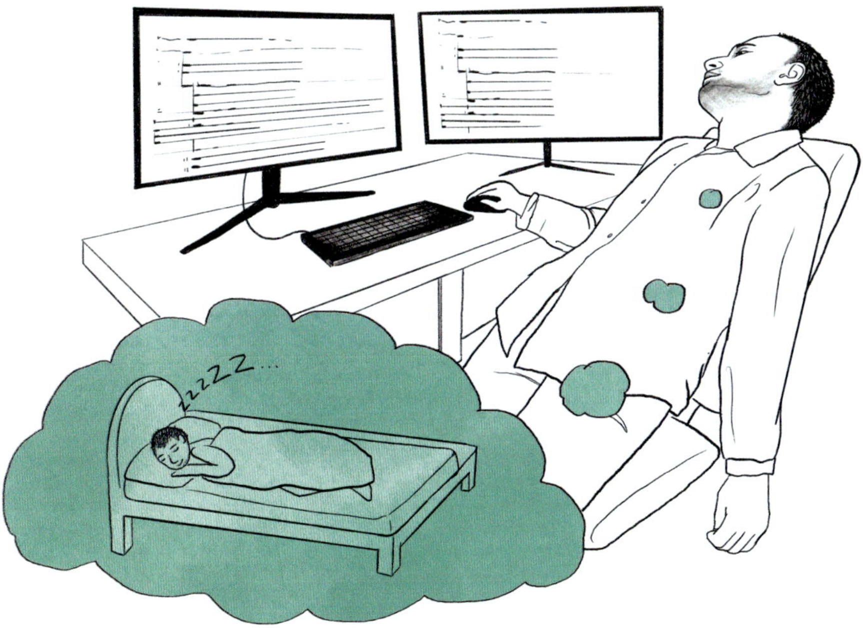

FIGURE 7.3 Crunch time.

of bliss turned into a bottomless abyss. She was not alone. Sondu left the house, kissing her goodbye.

Caspa turned around and began to run.

STEP 7.7 PUBLISH THE GAME

The first build of the pilot version was ready for publication. It was a great milestone, but the publication in the stores took longer than expected. The game was available as a web application and also available as a native app in the two biggest stores. The web application was stored on an external server under Chengs control and could be accessed by the target group via a browser, either on a computer or with a smartphone. The native apps required a bit more effort, since they needed to be uploaded to the stores and match specific requirements. The publication in one store went quite quickly, but the other one gave the team a hard time, causing additional iterations. Nonetheless, Cheng's team worked hard and was able to publish the game on time. There was just this one big bug somewhere hidden in the code that couldn't be resolved due to Cheng's illness. Caspa hoped that it wouldn't show up during the implementation. He ignored Daisy's calls, and when Prombu checked if everything was ok, he came up with a lame excuse. Everything was just too much. He couldn't focus on the game and didn't want to work on the necessary changes of the digital version, especially on the game design. He sat in his room and played a round of chess with his robot. He was about to lose.

"What do you think, Evali? Should we just quit?"

NOTE

1 Salen, K. & Eric Zimmerman (2004). Rules of Play. Game Design Fundamentals. Cambridge, Massachusetts: The MIT Press.

STAGE C

Implementation

CHAPTER 8

Phase 8

Piloting

It was Anaka who cheered him up. They sensed that something was wrong and visited the academy to support Caspa. Anaka was incredibly empathetic. Caspa lay on the ground of his darkened room in stasis. Anaka opened the curtains, a beam of light illuminated the room.

"I know that Daisy really likes you. Don't give up on her. Stay resilient. Also, this is your final project at the academy, and it means a lot to you. I heard about the loss of your parents, and I am terribly sorry. But now is not the time to surrender. Get back on your feed, Caspa."

Anaka reached out a hand to help him up. Caspa had tears in his eyes. He nodded and took it.

"You are right. Let's do this."

Anaka took him for a drive: "The pilot phase is the moment when our "baby" finally gets out of the protected testing cycle and is released into the real world, a big moment for the team. It might sound exaggerated, but I heard developers calling the game "their baby" countless times, which is no surprise given the ownership, commitment and personal investment they showed during the past months. Before allowing the serious game to conquer the world in the upscaling phase, we still are watching closely how it performs in the pilot phase. This phase is also called soft-launch, especially in commercial games. We usually select one smaller market that is similar to the bigger market that we are aiming for in the upscaling phase and implement the game there. In the pilot phase, we try to control

DOI: 10.1201/9781003461531-12

the environment as good as possible and gather data how the game performs. The phase also serves as a test to check whether it is worth investing more money in improving the game.

If your product is an analogue boardgame, your pilot phase might consist of implementing the game in a single university or a single company site of a global enterprise. Find the right size for your pilot implementation (Figure 8.1). Too small will not give you enough valid data and insights for the upscaling phase, too big and it might slip out of your hands. Either way, your team should be ready for what comes.

In many projects, directly before the official publish, the team goes through the crunch time phase. Some teams having a week or two of holidays in order to make up with the crunch time, and you can already take this time into consideration when planning your pilot phase. You will need the full capacity of your team when implementing the game, because no matter how good you tested, there will be emergency meetings on crucial bugs and problems to solve. If half of your team is in vacation, you might not be able to react immediately, which might put the success of the pilot phase at risk. Don't exploit your team, but everybody involved needs to understand that the pilot phase is crucial for the entire project.

FIGURE 8.1 Pilot implementation in one area.

The implementation of serious games is not only about distribution. We want to plug our game to a specific context and aim for real impact; we don't want to simply sell and distribute the game to as many people as possible. The creation phase empowered us with a tool, our game. Now it is time to actively use the game purposefully."

STEP 8.1 RUN A KICK-OFF EVENT

Caspa sat in the garden with Tesca and Anaka, discussing the kick-off event.

"The official launch of the pilot version is usually celebrated in a kick-off event. On the one hand, the kick-off event recognizes the efforts of the past, while on the other hand it initiates the actual implementation phase and is a major milestone. Important stakeholder will be part of it, and now is not the time for failures.

Having technical problems in this moment must be avoided at all costs. It has been shown that conducting rehearsals of the entire kick-off event can be of great benefit and, depending on the importance and complexity, even essential. It is like giving a concert. A lot of things can go wrong, especially if we have to use technology. As a rule of thumb, I try to run two rehearsals before an important kick-off, sometimes more. Try to resist the temptation to change anything essential between the final rehearsal and the kick-off event. I did this mistake twice, trying to do some last day changes to improve a small piece of the game, causing a major bug on stage. Trust me, you don't want this to happen.

Common sense prevails here, and you have to decide for yourself which last-minute changes are justifiable.

Have realistic expectations of your target group when they voluntarily attend an event and try to address this issue before it is too late. Think about how many exciting events, free webinars and digital meetups you would actually like to attend and receive invitations to, but only attend a fraction of it despite your interest or even your confirmation.

Finally, let us speak about credits in the kick-off event. The entire team has put a lot of work into the project over the past few months, and now is the official occasion to thank them for their efforts. Appreciation plays a big role in our lives, especially in our professional interactions. Depending on the size of the project, it is usually not possible to thank each person individually, but the individual teams and their part in the value creation process should be recognized. I would like to empathize the importance of

FIGURE 8.2 Appreciating the team in the kick-off event.

this point, as the whole team culture and atmosphere can be severely disrupted if people feel left out. Photos, videos and "behind the scenes" movies can be extremely rewarding, and you should make sure that all relevant project members are visually represented (Figure 8.2). At first glance, this may seem exaggerated, because after all, the team was just doing their job. However, serious games development is an artistic co-creative process, and all contributors deserve an appropriate appreciation, which also has a big positive effect on the team culture and cooperation for future projects.

Speaking about team culture. Tesca, could you show me the retro-museum? These two need a bit of privacy."

Caspa's heart stopped for a moment when he smelled the indescribable scent of Daisy. She put a hand on his shoulder, then sat next to him. Her presence was overwhelming.

"You rejected my calls, but I think we should talk."

STEP 8.2 CONSIDER CENTRAL AND DECENTRAL IMPLEMENTATIONS

The next morning, Caspa's mood was much better. He sat next to Daisy in a team meeting, listening to Prombu's explanation.

"Let's discuss central and decentral implementation. The term digital divide describes the persistent fact that not all people have equal access to the digital world, be it due to high costs for internet and devices, poor connectivity in rural areas, political and structural limitations, but also a lack of digital literacy, which means having skills and knowledge to navigate through and make use of digital opportunities.

In the analysis phase, we gained more knowledge about our target group and the context, and in the conceptualization and construction phase, we should have incorporated these limitations by realizing an inclusive game."

"Derren told me about it. In the implementation strategy, we need to be careful not to simply take the easiest route and aim for an implementation that relies exclusively on the easily accessible urban centres, even if the "numbers" are easier to achieve. We have to reach out to people living in rural areas as well, but how?"

"Let's talk about centralized, analogue implementations first, for instance implementing the game as part of trainings, conferences or promotional events. People from rural areas may not have sufficient motivation or resources to travel to a metropolitan area for our implementation event. Already in the framing phase, we can consider to allocate resources and support people with the transportation. After an application and selection phase, individuals could be enabled to travel to our central training site at project expense and, as an additional incentive, are reimbursed for accommodation.

The centralized implementation approach provides an opportunity for team building and forming multipliers. The participants have a shared task in a foreign environment, for instance mastering the challenges of a training and can grow together as a team. These individuals can become valuable experts, learn the subject matter in the central area to afterwards disseminate it in rural areas. This rarely happens by chance and should be planned from the outset in the implementation strategy, so how the roll out afterwards happens. The multipliers need to be empowered to not only apply but also disseminate the subject matter, teaching them how to teach. The advantage of centralized implementation is that we can establish a close connection to the participants and have access to infrastructure of the metropolitan area.

The decentralized implementation approach implies a different strategy. We can either travel from place to place, similar to a concert tour, and carry out our implementation activities there with a team of implementers. It is also an option to carry out the implementation events simultaneously at different locations at once, which requires increased coordination and the corresponding personnel. Depending on the project, however, this can have its own appeal and create a great sense of unity when analogue synchronous events are connected via the digital world.

The advantage of decentralized implementation is that we usually reach a larger audience and also choose a more inclusive design, as we create fewer hurdles for people from rural areas than in centralized implementation. Decentralized implementation is often associated with higher costs, coordination and logistical efforts. In fragile contexts, decentralized implementation can also pose a security risk for our traveling implementers. This must be evaluated in the framing and analysis phase and would have corresponding implications for our implementation.

Especially for digital serious games, we often have the opportunity to run an efficient decentralized implementation. If the game is designed and constructed inclusively, we can reach people in rural areas, even if we are operating in fragile contexts with low stability and security. Again, digital divide, digital literacy, gaming literacy and accessibility must be taken into consideration. Also be aware of the digital fatigue that we have observed, especially since the coronavirus pandemic. Digital decentralized implementation, without having a supporting implementation team at the physical space, requires successful promotion and marketing activities beforehand.

Thinking about a mix of centralized, decentralized and analogue and digital implementation is usually the way to go (Figure 8.3). Don't underestimate the efforts, coordination and logistical obstacles, budget and time that are required to run the implementation phase. Don't make the same mistake that I was doing in the past a few times, just constructing the game and then realizing that you ran out of resources to make the project a real success. This is nearly unavoidable without planning the implementation in advance. Now you know why we already set up the implementation strategy document in the creation stage."

The next days, Derren, Anaka, Daisy and Caspa conducted the analogue implementations of the physical game, with great success. The new students loved the way of developing their own serious games in the magic circle, while throwing process threats to their opponents. Prombu sensed a possibility to upscale the game to private companies who are interested in the development process. Caspa ignored the sword of Damocles, the

FIGURE 8.3 Examples for different implementations of serious games.

crucial bug in the digital pilot version that he had to take care of. Instead, he remembered Daisy's voice in his head:

"Sondu is an old friend of mine. We were never dating. In his culture, a quick kiss on the side of the mouth expresses friendship, not amorous feelings. I am still a bit annoyed by you ghosting me, I have to admit. Perhaps I will forgive you one day. If this happens, you can ask me out."

Her smile afterwards would be engraved in his memory forever.

STEP 8.3 ITERATE TO MASTER VERSION

The digital pilot implementation was a failure. Caspa thought that the test sessions were enough to guarantee a successful operation, but the reality proofed him wrong. The team had to conduct internal emergency meetings and release new builds on a daily basis. A lot of game design improvements and bug fixing were necessary. It wasn't a disaster, still Caspa was very disappointed. Confusingly, he saw the face of Prof. Monty in his mind's eye while hearing the stern voice of his father in his head: "You could have done more. You could have been better." These thoughts brought Caspa to the edge of despair. It was somehow funny. The entire time he was somehow jealous of Derren, but now it was him who recognized his inner conflict.

"Don't worry. The pilot version evolves into the master version. The pilot phase wasn't perfect for sure but still good enough. For private reasons, you feel low on energy now. But your team is there for you to back you up. Prof. Monty granted additional funds to iterate, and also Prombu told me that she found additional funding opportunities, so we can clearly upscale to the master version, which is a great success. Daisy and the rest of the team told me that they are excited to continue. We can work on debugging, but also should have a look at our product backlog and the features that are still on it. We have some ideas that could not be implemented for the pilot phase, but we also gained new insights from the implementations that will lead to the planning of new or adapted features. Furthermore, additional content of the subject matter should be integrated. Finally, we should start the localization to translate the game into new languages and adapt it to the new target audience that Prombu organised. The simultaneous AI translations are of great added value, still it needs to be checked by humans to do justice to the subtleties of languages. Here we need to have several meetings between the commissioners, producer and director to prioritize the next steps and identify what is doable in the construction time between the pilot phase and the upscaling phase. The discussed planning tools can help us to structure and prioritize the work again."

In the next days, they had many planning meetings with the commissioners, Prof. Monty and managers from private companies who want to make use of the game and the team to prioritize the next steps. Prombu raised an additional budget for marketing activities, which fell under Anaka's responsibilities. If they wanted to roll out the game on a big scale, investing in marketing and community building was mandatory.

STEP 8.4 CONSIDER PAID ADVERTISING

Caspa and Anaka were sitting on an observation deck of one of the seven big towers of the academy and planned the expansion of the marketing activities.

"If our serious game is placed in the stores, we have to compete against countless existing apps, and hundreds are added every day. In simple terms, paid advertising describes our marketing activities in which we pay an external platform or service provider to place our advertising. As large social media platforms have huge amounts of data at their disposal, they can target the audience very precisely. We can pay to advertise to a very narrow target group in several stages. For example, once a person has viewed our post for a certain amount of time, we define them as interested. In a second stage, all the people we have defined as interested will then receive another post a week later with further information. So, we throw a fishing lure into the sea of the social media platform, and the social media platform takes us on a metaphorical boat to the location where our target group is present. The fish that look at the bait with interest are lured with more bait until they eventually bite and click on the link. The more data there is about individuals on the web, the more tailored they can be addressed. And most people now have a very large digital footprint that the platforms can interpret and use. Paid advertising burns like a bright flash in the pan and requires a constant marketing budget.

Try to analyse and positively influence the breadth and depth of your campaign. Chansun Park[1] once had a great talk on that. The breadth shows us if the game is interesting for a wide audience. The depth gives us an insight into how much interest there is among our target group. How

- Cost Per Install (CPI): The CPI compares the expenditure of our paid advertising campaign with the resulting app installs. It shows how efficient our campaign is. The higher the value is, the worse our campaign is performing, for instance 1 USD per install. The CPI depends on the quality of our campaign, and also on the region and the competition on the target market. Graphic style, camera work and lighting have a particularly large influence on CPI. The combination of type and chosen game mechanics is also very relevant. For example, if you advertise your mobile game with a promotional video, it should be clear to the user in the first 3 seconds what the game is about and how they interact with their smartphone to solve the task in the game. Do they have to tap quickly, draw creatively, answer questions or make voice inputs in the game? If the user likes the core mechanics and the art style, you have a good chance that they will install the app.
- Install per Mille (IPM): When a person opens a platform and an advertisement becomes visible on the user's screen, this is referred to as an impression. The IPM now measures how many installs per thousand of these impressions result. The higher the value the better, for instance 50-100 IPM. The value provides an indication of the scalability of our project. The IPM is strongly influenced by the theme or setting of our game, which often is mainly responsible for the first impression that we have from the game. The more niche the setting is, the worse the IPM usually is.

- Churn Rate (CR): The CR describes the percentage of player who uninstall the game after a defined time frame, for example, 7 days, 30 days or a year. An early dropout could result from wrong expectations, a buggy game or a bad first-time user experience (FTUE). Furthermore, the CR allows us to spot drop out peaks after a certain amount of time, for instance 8 days. We could analyse what happens in the game after 8 days of playtime, perhaps there is a hidden bug or we should hook the player to the system with a new feature that we initially planned to give them after 12 days. The CR is also an important number for revenues to identify whether the marketing costs pay off.

many people are interested in the game and how strong are they interested in it? I would like to explain three key figures that can be relevant in that regard.

Reflect on your marketing activities also from an ethical point of view. Just aiming for quick numbers and quantity at all costs is usually not the way to go, try to build trust and gain a loyal target group. Therefore, paid advertising should be supported by organic advertising.

STEP 8.5 CONSIDER ORGANIC ADVERTISING

Organic advertising is a strategy that focuses more on long-term relationships. Depending on the project goals, a mixture of paid and organic advertising is often the way to go. In organic advertising, we aim for a genuine connection with the target group and focus on person-to-person interactions, even if these can take place digitally. This relationship requires trust, and the target audience must see an added value. The interaction will also result in a better rating by the algorithms of our content on most platforms, since the content seems to be relevant. The loyalty of our target group leads to personal recommendations, which is perhaps the most powerful form of advertising (Figure 8.4). To support this growth, we can integrate multipliers or ambassadors in advance who interact with our content and thus get the ball rolling. The multipliers will hopefully come from our high-quality organic advertising, and can also be brought into the group as insiders."

Caspa laughed: "Isn't that a bit like paid people sitting in the audience and start clapping so that the rest of the audience claps too?"

"Yes, a little. But perhaps clapping is not the right metaphor, rather starting a lively discussion in a public place. Taking the first step is not easy for many people, and the ambassadors encourage our target group

FIGURE 8.4 Organic growth of a community.

get active. Personally, I am a fan of organic adverting, as we can actively respond to the opinions and perspectives of the target group and achieve honest, long-term and quality relationships. Probably the most important aspect to achieve organic growth is community management, our next step to discuss.

STEP 8.6 PLAN YOUR COMMUNITY MANAGEMENT

Community management has become an essential part of marketing and is especially important in the serious games industry. Active communities are extremely valuable to us, not only because of the numbers but also through the exchange of feedback and even the creation of community content. However, it is not easy to build and moderate an active community, since it is a competitive market with many companies and projects that all want to have their community around their brand.

We can distinguish between project-driven communities and fan-driven communities. Especially working on sensitive topics in fragile contexts, well-moderated project-driven communities are a good option to maintain control. We should aim to establish a community with a collective sense of togetherness, the feeling of being part of something bigger.

As initiators and moderators of online communities, we are often shocked at how little interaction our efforts stimulate. Humans are energy efficient creatures, and responding to content requires energy, even clicking a thumbs up button. How often do you just quickly jump on an online platform, extract the info you need and then exit without leaving a comment or a contribution? The anonymity of the digital world reinforces this effort of leaning back, even if we consider the post relevant. It is tough to measure the impact that our project has on these so-called lurkers, and we have to set the right expectations regarding the interaction in the community. Nevertheless, there are techniques we can apply.

One option is the integration of ambassadors and multipliers who respond to our content, share it, create own content and get the ball rolling. Furthermore, participants in a community need to feel safe and valued. Creating posts yourself requires courage, especially, if the community is not anonymous and people feel judged. Moderators should reply to each post by the community, encouraging them to continue sharing their thoughts. Members need not overcome any technical obstacles or usability problems in order to make a contribution. We want to waste as little of our member's brain power as possible on the posting process itself, but rather focus on the content of the post.

There are communities that produce their own game content such as levels, create fan graphics and come up with their own stories in the game world. We can stimulate this interaction, but it needs to be planned carefully. It is unlikely that we'll be able to quickly create a new community, start a music contest and hope to be flooded with creative inputs. Members need to be cared for, valued and supplied with new content on a regular basis. Having a human person representing and moderating the community is

- Narrative content: Narrative content makes use of the world building and setting of the game. It could be written from the perspective of a character in the game, who might report about new features or a story progression in the game.
- Events and seasonal content: Especially in mobile games, the announcement of events and seasonal content is of high importance for live operations to keep players hooked. Content that is only available for a specific duration creates a sense of urgency in the player, at the same time shows that the game is still curated. Next to in-game events, you could announce content competitions or free subject matter webinars.

- Game updates: Information about new builds, technical patches, bugfixes and also about new gameplay mechanics or balancing measures. Next to the technical curation, the balancing is especially necessary in competitive games, to equalize strategies that can be exploited and therefore decrease the fun. Furthermore, inform your players on additional content, new levels and additional permanent subject matter.
- News on the overall project: Often in serious games projects, the game is just a piece of a broader solution mosaic. The community can be informed about further developments and milestones of the overall project, allowing for positive spill-over effects between the activities.
- Context Gossip: News about the region, facts about the local geography, highlighting socio-cultural aspects of the target audience or holidays, local food, local specialties, etc. have been proven to be very well received by my communities.
- Rumours: Especially in vivid communities, the creation of rumours can be a nice way to stimulate discussions among the community. Just posting the shade or contours of a new character or posting pictures of new levels without explaining it allows the community to guess what might come next. Rumours work well if the community actively cares about the game and is already hooked.

another way to stimulate activity, allowing to link the content to a human face. A posting and production schedule helps to structure content and ensures that fans receive content on a frequent basis. In serious games, we can categorize the type of content as follows.

Usually, the ex-coms specialist is responsible for the community. It should be aligned with the overall goals and targets of the project and in most projects, community building starts during the construction or focus testing phase. Depending on the marketing strategy, you can also start this process in the framing phase, if you want to inform your target group on the entire development process."

Caspa's pen flow over his notebook. "Communities should be moderated. Be it to address toxic members of the community, so called trolls, but also with malicious chatbots. Toxic and harming content needs to be handled. What about sensitive topics and fragile contexts? How can we ensure that the participants in our community are not penalized for their activity?"

"You raise a crucial point. Data protection and data security are very important, and as the operator of a community, it is our job to ensure this security. We also need to think carefully about what kind of personal data such as name or email address is visible to other members of the community. Imagine a project in a male-dominated society where other genders have fewer rights than men. If, for example, a female person makes a critical comment about the context in the community and our system settings allow conclusions to be drawn about the person's identity, either directly or indirectly, we may be putting this member in immediate danger.

No matter how careful we are, any system can be hacked and we need to think carefully about whether we allow or even encourage sensitive discussions in the community. A code of conduct or community guidelines can help to define rules that all members must agree to. In reality, just a few members will read these guidelines if they are longer than two or three sentences. Keep this into consideration while planning your community management to avoid doing direct or indirect harm on any members."

NOTE

1 Chansun Park 2022: Drawing attention to your game. IGDC 2022. https://youtu.be/he2RIfMeNNM?si=gnIxT67SVMEjABXz.

CHAPTER 9

Phase 9

Upscaling

WHILE ON HIS WAY to his appointment, Caspa was very nervous. He just had meeting with Prombu a few minutes ago: "Reaching the upscaling phase is another great success and should be appreciated accordingly. When scaling up a game, whether analogue or digital, the initial investment in terms of effort, time and costs now really pay off. Digital projects can be scaled quite easily, taking the localization into consideration and the adapted server structure for a large number of users. Usually, for single player games this is less of an effort as for multiplayer games. Analogue solutions can be scaled as well, but this requires additional manufacturing, distribution and transportation costs. If people have to moderate the game, for instance because it is part of a workshop, additional moderators must be trained to implement the game in additional contexts. Speaking of further contexts, I have great news. I initiated the discussion with ten additional companies, three of them were really interested and one already gave me the confirmation that they want to implement the game. No worries, I spoke to Monty before that, but he wants to clarify some details with you on the upscaling. At the end, he is the initial commissioner who funded the project. Just because having other opportunities doesn't mean that we should not include him in the upcoming developments. So, the team is counting on you!"

DOI: 10.1201/9781003461531-13

Caspa had the feeling to disappoint Monty, given the problems they faced in the first digital implementations. Monty and Caspa were walking through an avenue of apple trees. It was the favourite tree of his mother. The wind blew through the branches. A ripe apple fell to the ground.

"My dear Caspa, your project is running quite well so far, especially the analogue pilot was successful. The digital approach seemed to cause many problems for players from rural areas. They faced problems with older devices and also didn't understand all game mechanics, which is a problem you should have considered beforehand. But the worst thing is, that you used symbols that were culturally inappropriate for some people from the mountain sides. I expect you to work on these things and release a new build very soon."

Caspa nodded and had a lump in his throat.

FIGURE 9.1 Scaling up a serious game to additional areas.

"Nonetheless, the project is still very promising. Prombu already informed me that there are external companies interested in the approach. I will give you my permission to upscale it and generate income, but within certain limitations (Figure 9.1). We need to set up a memorandum of understanding.

STEP 9.1 SET UP A MEMORANDUM OF UNDERSTANDING

The memorandum of understanding (MoU) is a non-binding agreement based on mutual trust and respect. It often represents a preliminary stage to a binding contract. MoUs can be concluded and updated more quickly, especially if our partner institution follows bureaucratically lengthy processes for concluding contracts that do not represent day-to-day business. Depending on the sensitivity of the context, the partnership relationship and mutual trust, an MoU may be a more elegant solution compared to a binding contract with dozens of pages to cover all eventualities. We should identify the limits in which the team may further develop and use the game. Ultimately, the game should not be misused. This light checklist can help us in structuring our MoU.

- Monetization – Is the team allowed to make money with the game through additional implementations with other partners? Are they allowed to place in-game advertisement? What kind? Are they allowed to sell the game and if yes, for which price? Is a freemium model an option? Are they allowed to sell parts of the game on other platforms, for instance the visual assets?
- Data – How is data and personal data processed in the future? What kind of data security and privacy measures have to be taken? When is the data deleted? Is the team allowed to sell any type of data to externals?
- Copyrights – Who is the owner of the intellectual property (IP)? Who holds the rights on the assets, code, videos, subject matter content etc? Should the game make use of Creative Common (CC) licence model, or should it be marked as Open Educational Resources (OER)? Is the team allowed reuse code and assets for upcoming projects?
- Logos and Credits – Where and how should the logos and credits appear? Should they appear in the game only or also on websites, promotional material and social media activities? In which order?
- Updates – What kind of updates is the team allowed to do? How far may the game deviate from its original purpose? Can the content and subject matter be updated or replaced? Does an update need to be confirmed before publication? Is an additional do no harm assessment required?

These are just some examples that should be discussed. Many commissioners tend to restrict the teams too heavily on the upscaling and reuse of the game and related assets. However, having an MoU or even contract that ensures that the game is not diverted from its initial purpose usually leads to a win-win situation. This is especially true for development cooperation: A game can be far more sustainable and have a far greater impact if the team has the ability to capitalize on the game, keep it in the stores, promote it and do further implementations even after the initial funding period is over."

Monty and Caspa agreed on the content of the MoU, and Monty gave him free rein, as long as he would add the logo of the academy in the game. Furthermore, the game would be accessible for all enrolled students of the academy for free; therefore, Monty would provide additional support in the curation and maintenance.

The young developer picked up the fallen apple and took a bite.

STEP 9.2 MEET THE LOCALIZATION EXPERT

The teahouse was crowded, and the smells from the street were equally enchanting and unpleasant. There was a lot of noise, and it was not easy not to be overwhelmed by the new impressions. The hot tea tasted fantastic, and his counterpart took a deep drag from a water pipe that smelled of apples. He wore beautiful colourful robes in local fashion, and big dark eyes looked at Caspa from a tanned face (Figure 9.2).

"Thanks again for meeting me, Mr. Lochan. Prombu was arranging this meeting for us. Could you kindly tell me what is your task as a localization expert?"

Lochan laughed. "Straight to business, right? In my country, we usually first start with a shared tea and get to know each other. Another person may have taken your behaviour as an insult."

Caspa blushed as he perceived his cultural faux pax. "I am very sorry, I didn't mean to offend you."

Lochan waved it off: "No worries, that's why I am here. I worked with Prombu many times, and she already gave me an introduction to the project. I am happy to answer your question. Depending on the project and upscaling strategy, we have to deal with localization, in principle a contextualization to a new target group and a new environment. Localization primarily involves language. Depending on the game, this can be a big task, especially if the language belongs to a new language family, includes different characters or requires a different script direction. All texts and

FIGURE 9.2 The localization expert Lochan.

dialogues must be translated, as well as all system-relevant texts such as button labels and text feedback. Attention must be paid to grammatical differences, for instance: The feminine form in Arabic has a different form than the masculine form. The characters in the game would address our avatar differently, in case we allow the player to choose a gender. If the game includes voice recordings, these could be re-recorded in additional languages as well, however just having subtitles is a possible cost-efficient compromise. Advances in artificial intelligence have significantly simplified the process, but numerous errors still creep into the automatic translations, which have to be corrected by humans, especially if we want to publish the game in local languages in rural areas that are not well covered by AI.

In addition to the language itself, the game must be checked for the need of cultural adaptation. Texts and visualization can be interpreted differently and even perceived offensively. What is the norm in some cultures may be sanctioned in others. We had a game in which we used ghosts to guide the player through a certain level, and while the European target audience perceived the ghosts positively, part of the Arab target group perceived the ghosts as something very negative related to dark magic, so the scene in the game didn't work anymore.

Cultural adaptation goes hand in hand with any necessary examination of legal principles and religious nuances. Depending on the sensitivity of the content and the fragility of the context, thoughtless scaling into a context that perceives the game as offensive can have serious consequences for the implementation and even affect the personal safety of the people implementing it. Empathy, respect, expertise and knowledge of the political, religious and cultural foundations of the target context is required to enable a successful scaling. Consultation with local stakeholders or localization experts is therefore required to follow the do no harm mindset.

As the percentage of sugar of some drinks is adapted to the target market, games can also be adapted in its ingrediencies. If a game is successful in Scandinavia and should be upscaled to the Asian market, it may well make sense to adapt the visual game effects and music, the speed of the game and even entire game loops. Different cultures also have different learning cultures, so also the style of the subject matter integration can be adapted to suit the prevailing learning culture and enable better learning outcomes.

Many games already try to minimize written language in games and rely on symbols, which is especially true for analogue games that require the manufacturing of tangible material. Certainly, a good approach, also in terms of inclusion of people with a low level of literacy. However, symbols and their arrangement must also be checked for cultural appropriateness. Some symbols are acceptable and understandable in some cultures, while in other cultures the same symbol means something offensive or is simply not understood."

"Yes, Jake Manion mentioned that the owl in Europe stands for wisdom, while in the African context he implemented his game, the owl stands for death."

"A nice example. Localization is more than just translating the text of the game, it is about respecting and understanding the local culture. I am happy to help you localize the game to our context, so count me in."

STEP 9.3 CONDUCT IMPLEMENTATION WORKSHOPS

The localization with Lochan went flawless, however certain illustrations had to be adapted by Panita and Daisy adapted some rules of the game. Thanks to Prombu's good relationship with the manufacturer, the analogue game was ready to be published in the new context very soon. She organized a series of physical workshops in which an implementation team headed by Caspa conducted workshops on site. In contrast to official kick-off events with a lot of official speeches, the workshops were very tailored to the practical aspects on how the specific company could benefit from the use of serious games. Caspa's game *Crunch Time* served as a tool to give an overview about the development process. But next to this, he wanted to gamify the workshops a little bit. He heard of an insightful Mind Games Blink by the outstanding Alessia Messuti.

Caspa turned to Evali, but without saying anything, the robot already started the video.

GUEST BLINK ALESSIA MESSUTI, ITALY: IMPLEMENTING SERIOUS GAMES

As a Learning Innovation Officer for the past ten years at the International Training Centre of the International Labour Organization (ITCILO), a training institution belonging to the UN system, Alessia Messuti has felt honoured and privileged to conceive, design and develop learning solutions that were fit for the beneficiaries of this organization. Her work has been focusing on using the current trends in how people learn, and game-based learning is indisputably one of those trends. This helped Alessia to realize interactive learning products and experiences that are meaningful to the learners through setting up problem-based, scenario-based, collaborative and cooperative learning experiences and environments.

While in ITCILO, I made a considerable effort to understand gamification and serious games and where its application can extend the benefits of learning intended for adult learners. In essence, gamification and serious games served as an approach for the enrichment of a wide array of learning products, which extended from live face-to-face sessions and webinars to online self-guided modules and MOOCs.

Benefits of applying gamification and serious games in workshops are:

- Games by the employment of storytelling captured the interest of learners and motivated them to participate actively in the design of more engaging online learning experiences.
- Games have a scenario that needs to be solved, thus improving the critical thinking and decision-making skills in situations, for example, Labour Inspection. Simulating real-life situations, games help to enable people to apply theory in action while using knowledge and skills. As a result, it allows them to remember better and understand said information.
- In many of the games I designed, the very purpose was to promote teamwork and partnership, which are vital both on a professional and personal level. This is made possible, for instance, by online courses in which human connection is available and actively recommended.

But let's look into the process. As a learning designer, I think there are at least two basic points to consider when employing serious games:

- Learning objectives must be aligned with activities: It is very important that the two are somehow in harmony. Game elements and mechanics have to be introduced in such a way that they play the role of achieving educational objectives.
- Engaging design phase: if implemented correctly, including adapted game mechanics can make a remarkable difference in learner engagement. If design is the start, implementation is equally important as the actual interaction comes in the delivery – the moment that content goes in front of the end user. This is when the serious fun begins, and feedback becomes crucial. Therefore, implementation is a fun phase.

So how do you do this? How do you moderate and organize it so the implementation is successful?

Imagine to be in the classroom (physical or virtual). A cohort of learners are in front of you or even better, with you. Right now.

A gamified activity that I deliver quite often is a treasure hunt or scavenger hunt as I believe is a great energizer, it allows for cooperation and spatial exploration, it helps releasing endorphins through movement.

Tips for Successful Implementation

1. Use engaging storytelling to present the activity. Why a treasure hunt? Is the place where the activity will take place particularly relevant? Why do you want them to move around? Share a story about it. For example, where I work there is luckily a lot of outdoor space; therefore, I like to invite learners to think they are joining a tour, they are going to leave for a journey, they are coming from a different planet and therefore forced to look at the surrounding environment with new eyes. The use of metaphors helps captivating learners' attention, making the educational experience more memorable and enjoyable.
2. Share clear instructions: What do learners need to accomplish? Is there a specific goal? What is their mission? Make it short and clear. In the example of the treasure hunt, present in one slide the essentials such as the objective and basic rules: Find out as many "hidden gems" as possible in 30 minutes. This is your mission. Explain team composition rules. Highlight what is forbidden to do.
3. Provide clear incentives: Make clear since the beginning why is it important for them to join and play. Is it a matter of knowing

better each other and finding partners for future collaboration? Will they win a prize? I like to combine both intrinsic and extrinsic incentives: a small prize at the end such a book, a souvenir, a local food… But it should be clear that participating in this activity first of all helps them in learning.

4. Create the atmosphere: Play some music background which enhances the storytelling, provide them with handouts or items such as cameras, recorders, notebooks, etc. Learning is not about acquiring knowledge. Still, most importantly, about improving people's lives, making them comfortable. And this can only happen if people feel safe and enjoy what they do. Therefore, I would add two essential tips to the list, which are:
5. Include reflection spaces: In gamified live sessions, whether face-to-face or online, it is essential to create reflection spaces. These are moments where learners can honestly share their experiences, discuss what they found engaging and reflect on the particularly effective game elements. For both face-to-face and online, having a space for reflection is very important. This is where learners share what happened to them, what was the best thing. And most importantly if they can reflect on what game elements were beneficial and triggering for them. This aspect is particularly relevant if the audience is made of trainers, and therefore this gives them an opportunity to reflect on what worked and why for future replications of the same activity or strategy.
6. Include opportunities for real-time feedback: Embedding feedback mechanisms within the implementation phase allows immediate reflection and adjustment. This all helps in understanding the learners' needs and any obstacles they might be facing.

Conclusion

By aligning learning objectives with activities and embedding storytelling, atmosphere, reflection, instructions, feedback mechanisms in the implementation phase, we can ensure that learning is engaging, effective and enjoyable. This not only facilitates knowledge acquisition but also raises the quality of a learner's life to be comfortable, secure and motivated.

STEP 9.4 TAKE CARE OF GAME CURATION

The digital master version was finally ready to go. It improved a lot since the initial pilot phase was about to get implemented in a variety of contexts. But this didn't mean that the work for the team was over. Cheng appreciated that the budget planning included a comprehensive game curation.

"Most projects make the huge mistake of not allocating budget for this phase. Especially digital games are like a sensitive houseplant: They will die without irrigation and curation (Figure 9.3). Let me explain what I understand by curation.

- Maintenance – Work required to keep the game online and functioning in its status quo, mainly consisting of programming work. This includes debugging of bugs that occur while the game is published, and also in adapting the game to new requirements from the stores and platforms. It also incorporates the costs and efforts necessary to curate the server and communication between the server and devices.
- Balancing – Improvements on the game design, especially in competitive games. New builds are released on a regular basis to balance the gameplay and game values and eliminate strategies that are out of control and reduce the fun.
- Major Updates – Work that take the game beyond its status quo. This may consist of big gameplay and feature updates, new levels, narratives or additional subject matter.
- Live Ops – If a game is planned to receive frequent updates, events, seasons and a very vivid community, the game is in live operations. Some teams call the entire uspcaling phase simply "live ops", especially in the commercial sector. However, I prefer seeing it as a strategy and design decision. Decide on how much budget for live ops can be allocated, having a team that is working on improving the game for and with the community, regularly providing them with events and major updates.

Due to the MoU agreement with Prof. Monty, Prombu was able to raise funds for game curation with a considerable budget for live ops and monetize the game through digital and analogue implementations for private companies. Next to maintaining the game in the stores, Daisy balanced the game on a frequent basis, Derren, Tesca, Dr. Sumato and the artists developed major gameplay updates, enriching the game with more features and subject matter. Cheng and Caspa took care of the live ops and designed seasonal events and temporary content on a frequent basis.

It was a lovely summer day, Daisy and Caspa had a walk through the park. Now it was about time. He tried to find the right words, but was interrupted by her warm voice.

FIGURE 9.3 Serious games without curation.

"We made it. The game is having some real impact, training people all around the world on serious games development. They can use them to make the world a better place. Sustainability is such an important topic, and I know a wonderful Mind Games Talk by the splendid Eyram Tawia. Would you be so kind, Evali?"

GUEST BLINK EYRAM TAWIA, GHANA: LONG-TERM IMPACT AND SUSTAINABILITY IN SERIOUS GAMES

As CEO and Co-founder of Leti Arts, with over 20 years of experience in game development and gamification projects, Eyram Tawia has dedicated his career to enriching African storytelling through interactive games and comics. This chapter explores his personal journey as a game developer and studio owner, managing numerous serious game projects and catering to diverse clientele. Eyram speaks about sustainability of gamification projects post-production, a critical aspect of the long-term impact of serious games. Additionally, he will examine how engaging in gamification projects influences studio structure, driving innovation and adaptation in internal processes, ultimately transforming gamification efforts into viable products or services.

Often, clients engage gaming experts and studios to develop games for specific advocacy efforts but lack insight into what a game truly is and how it lives after creation. The initial focus is typically on the notion that "kids love games" and will readily engage with educational content if presented in a game format. While this sentiment serves as a starting point for collaboration, it is imperative for clients to gain a deeper understanding of the entire process and trust the expertise of gaming professionals to guide them effectively.

Sustainability is key once a game is made. In the gaming industry, this is referred to as "live ops." Most impact games are used for research purposes and are not intended to have a long shelf life on digital stores. However, from my experience with serious games, differ in this regard. I have seen many serious games on digital platforms remain neglected for years without updates because clients often do not allocate sustainability budgets. I have encountered several instances where projects, my studio developed for significant clients were eventually abandoned on digital stores and deleted by platforms like Google due to a lack of sustainability planning.

My experience in developing games in Africa presents its own challenges, making it even more disheartening to see these projects fail due to inadequate sustainability planning. To address these issues, my studio has devised strategies to counsel clients on allocating sustainability and marketing budgets. Some clients opt to separate production bids from marketing and support bids, adhering to open tender policies while acknowledging the need for ongoing support and promotion. Also, most of my clients often intrude on the design process, skewing the game to fit their understanding, which can reduce the game's educational impact. It is crucial for clients to trust the expertise of gaming professionals who know how to seamlessly integrate learning into gameplay.

My studio has innovated around these challenges by engineering a tech license model that encompasses development, customization, and ongoing support. In this arrangement, the client owns the final product but not the underlying game infrastructure, which is derived from years of technological development. The license covers the cost of using our technology and hosting the game on our servers, including free updates to the framework. Maintenance covers live ops and bug fixes, ensuring the game remains operational and up-to-date. This way, the studio is protected with a budget to keep the game running and is held accountable to ensure its smooth operation. If a client wants all the tech for themselves, they pay a one-time license fee that includes the source code and are free to deploy it on their servers, using us or any other provider for maintenance. This process encourages clients to view their game not as a one-time project but as a sustainable one with a tech service behind it. This may also include all monitoring and evaluation requests to track the game's impact.

Navigating the world of serious games has been a rewarding journey, though personally, it remains challenging to help clients understand what a game truly is. In the game development community, we often say, "making a game is no fun." Being a game player does not necessarily mean one would enjoy making a game. My clients often realize this only after experiencing the extensive work required to bring a game to life. From the processes outlined in the earlier chapters of this book, it becomes clear that game development is a long process from pre-creation to post-implementation. Throughout this development process, sustainability considerations should be seamlessly integrated.

During pre-creation, collaboration with clients and subject matter experts defines the game's objectives and content. The creation phase focuses on bringing the game to life, while sustainability efforts become critical in the latter stages of development, ensuring the game remains relevant and impactful long after its initial release.

I know you would be wondering what happened to the numerous games my studio has worked on which haven't had sustainability budgets in the past. When do we kill those projects? When do we say enough? We typically decide to end such game's lifecycle once the research or data collection period is over, especially for serious games designed for such purposes. If the project lacks a sustainability budget, we keep it available for reference purposes at our own cost until we can no longer invest in it, at which point we remove it from the store.

The journey of developing serious games, particularly within the challenging landscape of Africa, has been both rewarding and fraught with obstacles. I have witnessed firsthand the transformative potential of serious games in education, advocacy, and social change. However, the path to creating lasting impact is intricate, demanding a deep understanding of game development beyond mere creation.

Conclusion

Ultimately, I would say the key to successful serious games lies in collaboration, trust, and a commitment to sustainability. My advice to project managers and clients is that, they must learn to trust gaming experts and avoid taking over the design process, which can most times jeopardize the success of serious games. Understanding and planning for sustainability is crucial to ensuring your serious game achieves its intended impact and remains a valuable educational tool over time. Clients must recognize that

> games are a unique medium requiring specialized knowledge and continuous support. By fostering a deeper understanding and respect for the game development process, we can create serious games that truly make a difference. My journey in this industry has underscored the importance of this approach, and I hope it serves as a guiding principle for project managers and clients alike. Trust in your gaming experts, and together, we can achieve remarkable outcomes.

The blink was amazing, and while the two slowly returned to the academy, Caspa couldn't wait any longer: "Without the team and their individual strengths, I couldn't have made it this far. The project wouldn't be the same without them. But you are the one who changed my life. I felt it the first time I saw you on the island. You are the most intelligent, beautiful, and creative person I know. I would never forgive myself if I didn't dare to ask: Daisy, will you go out with me?"

STAGE D

Post-Implementation

CHAPTER 10

Phase 10

Reflection

WHILE SITTING IN A long-distance train, Caspa watched the environment as it flew by at high speed. The surroundings blurred, and he saw pictures and scenes from his journey in his mind's eye. He recognized his parents and how it all started. How he created the high concept note and getting to know Monty, Prombu, Derren, Anaka, Dr. Sumato and Tangesh from the target group in the desert. He remembered when he fell in love with Daisy, met Panita and Sondu on the tiny island, travelled to the underwater city to meet Cheng and onboarding Tesca back in the academy, creating and testing the game in the creation stage. Caspa remembered his chess play with Evali and how the process and his heart crushed through the change of requirements, the crunch time and the kiss of Sondu and Daisy.

As a team, they mastered the challenges of the bumpy road of the implementation stage, and Caspa remembered Anaka's hand helping him up. He tasted the tea with Lochan when they upscaled the game into many new contexts. Caspa and the entire team evolved through this project, and he felt blessed that he was part of it. His parents would be proud of him. He contributed to global good by giving upcoming developers the tools they need to support the idea of NESGA, contributing to the holistic net that spans the earth and working on environmental, social, good governance

DOI: 10.1201/9781003461531-15

as well as animal-related topics to ultimately fight climate change and reduce natural disasters.

After five years, the funding from Prof. Monty was about to end, so Caspa and the team had to evaluate the project.

STEP 10.1 EVALUATE YOUR DATA

Since evaluation was an integral part of the entire project, Prombu and Derren set up the impact systems already in the framing phase. These systems allowed to extract short-impact reports that now would play an important role for the final report. They evaluated direct, indirect, quantitative and qualitative data aiming for a 360-degree impact measurement.

Prombu, Derren and Caspa sat in the Sus-Tower, and reflected on the data. The senior producer was very confident.

"We collected sufficient direct in-game data through the impact measurement systems, conducted interviews, evaluated questionnaires, in-game and out-game experiments, real life challenges and tried to evaluate indirect data, keeping in mind the ripple effects that resulted at least partially from the project. The data is great, but we have to be aware that our implementations were no closed experiments in the academy. We implemented the game in the beautiful chaos of reality. There is a wonderful Mind Games Talk by the tremendous Dr. Bastian Laier. Evali, please play the video!"

GUEST BLINK DR. BASTIAN LAIER, GERMANY: SERIOUS DATA

Dr. Bastian Laier has been working in research and teaching for over 10 years, specializing in quantitative methods of social research. Whether in the scientific community, the business world or in areas of public life, the evaluation of projects and other plans has been an integral part his life.

Evaluation is not just about looking at whether a particular result has been achieved. A well-planned evaluation can be seen as an ongoing process. It provides valuable information about current and future progress. I would like to draw your attention to a few selected areas that may cause problems that you do not automatically think of when you first start collecting user data. Of course, I will also show you ways in which you can counter these potential challenges.

The first thing I would like to point out is something that surprised me when I first started collecting data: ***people can perceive questions very differently***. Depending on how you phrase a question, it can affect the answer in different ways. This doesn't necessarily mean that the answer will be wrong – although that can happen (!) – but depending on how and what you ask, it can trigger different perceptions and cognitive processes in respondents. Let's illustrate this with a small example. Let's assume that you want to ask your players how many friends they have who also play the game. At first glance, a simple and innocuous question. But you should be aware that friendship is not a definite state. When does a friendship exist? Do you have to know each other in real life? How often do you have to be in contact with each other? People give very different answers to these questions and therefore define friendship very differently. For some, a prerequisite for friendship is that you share your deepest secrets, while for others, it is enough to play an online game together every now and then.

Be aware of this and try to test the questions you want to ask in advance. For example, ask a friend – no matter how you define it – how they understand your questions. If something is unclear in your wording, you still have the opportunity to react and adjust the questions again.

Let's imagine another simple task: At the beginning of a game, you want to ask the age of the players. Simple, you say, just ask how old they are... but is it that simple?

Perhaps you've already noticed this in yourself: When someone asks me how old I am, I usually have to think for a moment because my current age is not particularly firmly anchored in me. After all, it changes from year to year and even varies within a calendar year. I prefer to occupy myself with other things rather than follow this rapid development. Of course I can give my correct age after a moment, but the point is that I came to a brief standstill and had to use a little more brain power than expected. But maybe that's just me. However, we know from research that there are also people who don't like being asked their age. In general, and this is your takeaway message, this is something we want to avoid when we ask someone questions that are important to us. ***Try to make the survey as non-annoying and easy to complete as possible***.

This small example illustrates one point in particular. Our first intuition about how to ask a question may be wrong. Instead of trusting our gut instinct, we should base decisions on the best available knowledge we have. In fancy words, we should make evidence-based decisions. And to do so, we need to read up on some research.

But don't worry, you don't have to read up on all the literature on evaluation or survey design to collect user data. You can tackle one problem at a time and always learn something new along the way that you might need for other upcoming tasks. Think of it as a toolbox that you can fill with different tools for different needs and that grows over time.

Another point I would like to address concerns the target group of your survey. Depending on the age, nationality, cultural background or other attributes, we may need to adjust our approach. Here's a little fun fact to illustrate the problem. Studies on life satisfaction often show that Japanese respondents generally report a relatively low level of life satisfaction, which is puzzling against the background of objective criteria such as the Human Development Index (HDI). Countries with similarly high HDI values generally also have a higher level of life satisfaction. So why are Japanese people so dissatisfied with their lives? The simple answer to this question is probably: They are not! One possible explanation is that this difference is due to cultural aspects, such as a requirement for modesty. Japanese people are perhaps simply too humble to show how happy they are with their lives.

What do we do with this knowledge? On the one hand, we can see that we should anticipate such circumstances and take them into account when analysing the data and, on the other hand, it shows us a general problem with such data: We can only very rarely be sure that we are getting correct answers. However, this is not game over for the collection of this data, but rather a particular challenge. ***Think about your target group in advance of your data collection.*** What is its composition? Are there any special features that you need to take into account? Try to get as clear a picture as possible of who you will be interviewing and take this into account when evaluating your data.

The last thing I want to point out must be faced with all honesty. Often you want to improve the world with a serious game and ideally you want to prove this with figures. Especially in reports to funders, you may be tempted to offer proof of the effectiveness of your work.

And here, too, it may seem simple at first glance. Let's say you've created a game that aims to increase players' knowledge in a certain area. To prove its effectiveness, you have the players take a quiz before the game starts and one after it ends. You assume that an improvement from the entrance to the exit test must be the effect of your game.

Let's imagine two settings for this example. In one, a training session takes place in which the players take an entrance test on site, then play the game and take an exit test immediately afterwards. In this case, the possibility for unobserved influences is rather limited and the difference between the two tests can probably be attributed to playing the game. In the other setting, on the other hand, players download the game and play it as they see fit. A lot can happen between the entrance and exit test that you cannot control. There are many parameters that you have not or could not take into account. For example, it is conceivable that your players were already interested in the topic and therefore got involved in the game in the first place, a so-called selection bias, and the observed effect is at least partly due to your players' own initiative. It's understandable that you're proud of your game and the desire for it to work is understandable, but don't overdo it if you can't be sure. Another pitfall of such tests could be that the questions in the initial and exit tests may present different difficulties. Any resulting improvement would therefore merely be an artefact of our survey method. Generally speaking, you should make sure that the entrance and exit tests are of comparable difficulty.

As a rule, reality is too complex to be captured in its entirety with our surveys. However, this should not discourage you from including such questions, but rather you should be aware that these possibilities exist. Ultimately, we can only capture sections of reality while others remain unconsidered. We therefore need to think in advance about what the most important aspects are for us and the project in question. ***Make a list of the information you want to collect and prioritize it.*** Consider various parameters that could have an influence on the results of questions and decide whether there is a way to take these into account directly or at least when evaluating the data.

Conclusion

In summary, all I am saying is that you should aim for an informed approach. ***If you want to create a serious game, then you should take every aspect of your game seriously, including the evaluation and collection of data***. As in all areas of life, there's always something to learn, and the mountain always looks steepest at its base. Once you've gone part of the way, you'll look back and realize that you've already achieved a lot and that gives you confidence to go the rest of the way, and that makes you a better evaluator and game designer in the long run.

STEP 10.2 CONSIDER THE USE OF THE MIND GAMES EVALUATION FRAMEWORK

Derren took the word: "Next to measuring the impact of a serious game, it can be useful to evaluate the quality of serious games itself. I developed the Mind Games Evaluation Framework to evaluate serious games either individually or to compare games on a specific topic. For instance: Which is currently the best serious game on animal migration? The tool can also be used to evaluate games of hackathons and game jams, and can already serve in the game concept phase as a self-check and reflection tool.

The framework evaluates six categories consisting of different evaluation criteria. Criteria or even entire categories can be removed or weighted differently with a maximum sum of 100%. For instance, we might not be able to gain details on external games on their impact measurement systems and therefore weight the entire category with 0%. Especially for game jams, the jury can also just evaluate the category as a whole, without giving single points for each criterion. Multiplying the weighting with the rating will lead to a score, adding up the category scores will lead to a ranking.

Mind Games Evaluation Framework (MGEF)

ID	Category or Criterion	Weighting (0–100%)	Rating (0–10 points)	Score
A	**Category A: Game Experience**			
A1	Overall game design			
A2	Game balancing			
A3	UX and usability			
A4	Atmosphere and immersion			
A5	Narrative			
B	**Category B: Technical aspects**			
B1	Performance/framerate			
B2	Bugs and glitches			
B3	Fidelity/audio and visual quality			
C	**Category C: Didactical approach**			
C1	Integration of subject matter into game experience			

(Continued)

Mind Games Evaluation Framework (MGEF)				
ID	**Category or Criterion**	**Weighting (0–100%)**	**Rating (0–10 points)**	**Score**
C2	Interaction with subject matter			
C3	Variety of subject matter formats			
C4	Clear relevance of the subject matter to the player			
C5	Connection to existing skills and assumptions			
D	**Category D: Ethics, Inclusion, Equity and Diversity**			
D1	Inclusion of diverse player groups			
D2	Variety of perspectives			
D3	Avoidance of addictive design			
D4	Transparency and reliability			
D5	Aspects related to sustainability			
E	**Category E: Accessibility and Scale Up Opportunities**			
E1	Design for disabled and illiterate persons			
E2	Overcoming language barriers			
E3	Affordability, pricing and price-performance ratio			
E4	Overcoming digital divide and limited internet access			
E5	Scale up potential			
E6	Accessibility for a wide range of devices and platforms			
F	**Category F: Impact Measurement Systems**			
F1	Direct quantitative impact measurement			
F2	Direct qualitative impact measurement			
F3	Indirect impact measurement			
F4	Data security, management and monitoring			
F5	Data access and control for users			
G	**Category G: Further Requirements**			
G1	Additional criterion			

The effectiveness of gamification and serious games was studied and evaluated by the astonishing Dr. Marigo Raftopoulos, who summarized her findings in a thrilling Mind Games Blink.

GUEST BLINK DR. MARIGO RAFTOPOULUS, AUSTRALIA: THE HEART OF GAME DEVELOPMENT

Dr. Marigo Raftopoulos founder of Strategic Innovation Lab is a strategy consultant with a PhD in enterprise gamification. She has worked with organizations globally to reframe approaches to creativity and innovation. She has recently completed an EU-funded Marie Curie Research Fellowship on her project Augmented-Humans, which focuses on how people and organizations can reinvent human-machine relationships in the age of artificial intelligence.

Creating a game is creating an interactive short story about life. Since ancient times, humans have learned from each other through stories, dialogue and games. The only thing that has changed over time is the technology we use – what lies at the heart and soul of humanity has stayed the same. The heart of the games we develop needs to reach and touch people with stories they can relate to.

At the beginning of my journey into gamification and serious games, I was convinced that games will change the world and help us solve problems that our current systems couldn't fix. But one day I got a reality check. An executive from an entertainment games company called me to visit him in his office in New York City. He heard about my work and research into gamification and asked if I could come and explain it all to him. After listening to me and asking a lot of questions he went quiet and was thinking about everything I had said. He then turned to me and asked thoughtfully, "So you think life, business, and society should get inspiration from games?"

I instantly felt like the conversation was going to take a turn. This was an intelligent man, his company had sold billions of dollars worth of entertainment games on the global market, and he was leading one of the most successful games companies in the industry. I was a bit confused – what couldn't he understand I wondered? He then said to me, "It's funny 'cos our game designers get their inspiration from everyday life."

It was then that it occurred to me that we were overfocussing on the tools and the technology to help us overcome what we had lost touch with – human-to-human dialogue and connection.

I ran a longitudinal study several years ago that tracked the performance of various serious games and gamified applications over a five-year period.[1] There were some very important findings from the companies that I surveyed that I'd like to share with you here. These companies did a lot of research and tested many different games and gamification initiatives in their organizations, so there are many important lessons to keep in mind as you progress on your creative journey:

- Be clear on the strategic value proposition. Designers and consultants need to better target and communicate with organizational leadership teams to generate high-level buy-in. Often gamification and serious games projects are initiated at the middle-management level and fail to reach high-level support. Illustrative quote: "Focus less on the tactical aspects and more on the strategic ones such as systemic changes and business transformation."
- Be professional. Several organizations stated that while the fun and engaging aspects of a gamification project were attractive, it started to wear thin and it became apparent that there was limited business expertise and substance behind their designer's capability. Illustrative quotes: "We're never inviting game developers here again" and "Gamification is not the holy grail of engagement; we expect that consultants and designers have a deeper knowledge of related business tools and approaches to support the project."
- Use fact-based assessments. Several mentions were made that gamification should be treated as a design discipline and needs to incorporate several layers of research, stakeholder involvement and strategic design. Illustrative quotes: "Stop throwing around case studies which are not validated or keep pushing the same old solutions" and "There's much more research around now, there needs to be more of it."
- Don't overpromise. Several organizations complained that many consultants and designers overpromised and underdelivered. Organizational challenges cannot be solved by games and gamification alone and designers need to understand and communicate their limits. Illustrative quotes: "Stop promising the world!" and "The game is never the overall solution, it's only part of the solution."
- Full-service product offering. Several organizations claimed that many designers and consultants were overly focused on the technology, that is, platform vendors or game developers, whereas their organization was looking for full-service offerings that included strategy, design and process transformation to ensure that the serious game was set up for success. Illustrative quotes: "Our project failed as it was difficult to integrate" and "There needs to be a clear understanding of which areas can be gamified and which shouldn't."
- Research is everything. There is a key difference between game designers and gamification/serious game designers. I love the freedom that entertainment game designers have. They are creative,

whimsical and very imaginative. However, for serious games we need to be mindful of data and facts and how we transfer that knowledge to people effectively and ethically.

According to Tracy Fullerton,[2] a wonderful game designer and educator, the fundamental role of the game designer is to be the "advocate of the player." This means that the designer must view the game world they are creating through the eyes of the game player. Their full focus needs to be on the player experience without being distracted by the other concerns of production.

Here is the disconnect between the role of a game designer versus the role of a serious game or gamification designer. A serious game or gamification designer is often the advocate of management, an institution or an investor. The focus on the player tends to be subordinate in the game they are developing to meet business requirements or a lesson to be learned.

The engagement and experience of the player in a gamified enterprise application is typically a means to an end (business outcome), rather than the end in itself such as fun and enjoyment. It is this clear distinction between these two positions, and the tension that arises from it often creates the need for compromise.

For this reason, a high-level "game thinking" approach is important to ensure the designer is an advocate of the player as much as an advocate of management. The challenge is to find an equilibrium between these two positions. For this reason, you need to trust the process of serious game and gamification design to find that win/position.

Given the nature of digital technologies, any serious game design framework must include a means to evaluate ethics as a key design consideration. Ethics has become a key area of concern for gamification researchers due to the problems that arise from dark design patterns. This is where interfaces and gameplay trigger behaviour at the subconscious level and is rife in gambling applications. Remember that games are not innocent – they reflect our mindsets and worldviews. Games can be used by both terrorists and humanitarian organizations with equal success.[3]

Conclusion

Let me now finish where we started. The New York game developers may get their inspiration from real life, and none of their games helped people reimagine how life could be better or different, they just provide a distraction. Their games kept people where they were, doing more of the same, and used design techniques to keep them grinding under the illusion of progress and autonomy. That's a design trick and it's manipulative. When I told this to the game's executive, he just smiled and said, you're absolutely right.

STEP 10.3 SUBMIT THE FINAL REPORT

The final report is an important artefact to evaluate whether the project was a success, failure or something in between. It is either done by the project team or external evaluators. As mentioned, the evaluation is an integral part of the entire process and this step doesn't describe its start, but its end. A structure of the final report could look like this:

- Project overview – Summary of the project including duration, costs and impact.
- Project description – Description of the project background, stakeholders and context.
- Target group – Summary of target group, market and context.
- Game description – Comprehensive overview about the game and its core features.
- External impact – Comparison between impact intension and actual impact.
- Team – Team behind the project and supporting stakeholders.
- Internal impact – Impact on the team internally and capacity building measures.
- Process – Process description and duration.
- Finances – Costs, revenues and value creation.
- Lessons learned – Major failures and what to learn from them.
- Recommendations for the future – Next steps and recommendations for upcoming projects.
- Appendix with detailed data – Proof of impact through direct and indirect data.

Obviously, the report can be enriched with additional chapters depending on the project and the needs of the recipient. I am personally in favour for it can contain text, pictures, videos, audio recordings, etc. The final report often represents the final artefact required to close a project."

Luckily, Evali accompanied Caspa for almost the entire process. It was full of data and recordings and its generated summaries were pure gold while writing the report. Caspa petted his cute robot.

That's why Prombu gave you to me as a present in the beginning. You were part of the entire journey, evaluating everything we did!" Evali beeped merrily (Figure 10.1).

FIGURE 10.1 The evaluation expert Evali.

STEP 10.4 HANDOVER THE GAME

Prombu continued: "To create sustainable games, you should consider a handover strategy already at the very beginning of the project, ideally in the framing phase. I experienced too many projects that didn't think of this step in advance and therefore just died when the initial funding stopped. For instance, handing over games for global good to local development studios can result in higher ownership and better results, leading to a win situation for the commissioner, the local studio and also the target group. An MoU or contract is usually needed to clarify the specifics of the handover, for instance how the studio may modify the initial purpose of the game or how it can monetize the game. Especially in development cooperation, too many project managers are hesitant to handover the project and allow for monetization, leading to a quick death of the game. Is has many advantages if the studio working on the game already knows from the beginning, how they can take over the game after the initial funding. In our case, Prof. Monty handed over the game to us, and see what happened."

"Sustainability through ownership. That makes a lot of sense. Eyram Tawia spoke about it in his Mind Games Blink. To develop products for longevity, the studio receiving the project should see an added value in curating the game, also from a financial point of view."

NOTES

1 Raftopoulos, M. (2020). Has gamification failed, or failed to evolve? Lessons from the frontline in information systems applications, GamiFIN Conference 2020, Levi, Finland, April 1–3, 2020.

2 Fullerton, T. (2008). *Game Design Workshop: A Playcentric Approach to Creating Innovative Games*. Burlington, MA: CRC Press.

3 Raftopoulos, M. (2014). Towards gamification transparency: A conceptual framework for the development of responsible gamified enterprise systems. *Journal of Gaming & Virtual Worlds*, 6(2), 159–178.

CHAPTER 11

Phase 11

Closure

EIGHT YEARS WENT BY after he met her. Caspa sat with his beautiful wife on their veranda, listening to the waves of the open sea. Evali was surely outdated, and Caspa just couldn't get away from it. It projected the latest numbers of his first professional game *Crunch Time*. He puffed and knew it was about time.

STEP 11.1 RECYCLE VALUE MODULES

Daisy smiled at him, and the developer still felt the enchantment by her fascinating presence. Caspa already knew what she was going to say. "It's about time, my love. Sooner or later, the product lifecycle of a game is over and it is on the way to its grave. That's ok, let it go. At a certain point, the circumstances of the environment have changed too much. The adaptation and additional investments to keep the game alive cost more than the value it creates. This could have happened both if we kept the game on our own team or if we would have done a handover to another studio. Let's inform our players that the game will no longer be supported. We have to keep into considerations legal issues and contracts, for instance checking on companies which bought the game and expect curation and maintenance. Furthermore, keep in mind the data privacy guidelines, we might need to delete personal data from all servers and inform the players about it. Take the game from the stores, but keep it in our portfolio. We learned

DOI: 10.1201/9781003461531-16

a lot from the project, and even if it is no longer public, it can serve as a reference for future projects."

Caspa nodded. He was no scholar anymore and became a professional game producer with many projects under his supervision, and some of them were steered by Daisy as creative director. *Crunch Time* as their first shared project would always owe a special place in their portfolio.

Daisy continued: "Next to the elimination, think about re-and upcycling parts of the game. I call them value modules (Figure 11.1). Perhaps we can re-use the subject matter, art assets, code or features of the game in upcoming projects? What did we learn from the game design? Perhaps we can reuse some core game loops and its balancing by just adjusting it to the next project? Even working narrative arcs can be recycled for future projects and reintegrated into a new setting. The game is still full of value that we shouldn't ignore. Following this step to explicitly extract and secure the value modules will increase the efficiency of our team. Reuse and adapt the modules in upcoming projects."

FIGURE 11.1 Recycle and upcycle value modules.

On the jetty, a pelican caught a fish, but this time swallowed it. Caspa agreed. "We could also sell the value modules on certain online platforms, for instance the graphical assets and music, and establish a passive income stream with the game even after its death. Another consideration would be the publication of the modules or the entire project for free, supporting the Open Educational Resources initiative.

We should avoid to eliminate and burry our game in the depths of a messy folder structure, without making use of its hidden values."

Carefully, Evali crouched out of sight.

STEP 11.2 CLOSE THE PROJECT

Prombu reunited the old project team and invited Prof. Monty to the academy, who was in well-deserved retirement. They sat together in the great *interactivum*, the students enjoyed their winter holidays. Caspa's new scholar handed a cup of coffee to Sondu, when Prombu took the word.

"The time has come to close this wonderful project. We made a final re-organization of the project repository, cleaned up the files and made sure that upcoming co-workers and students can access and learn from the project (Figure 11.2). We ran a few internal team retrospectives of the project, reflecting on lessons learned and how to improve collaboration and teamwork in the future. We made an honest reflection with all ups and downs, yet ended on a very positive note, even if the project was

FIGURE 11.2 Close the project and take the lessons learned into the future.

challenging. We created a constructive atmosphere with a team that evolved and still is excited to take on challenging projects in the future.

We communicated the project closure to the community and to all relevant stakeholders. We made a clear and transparent cut and explained, why the project was ending. Very similar to the kick-off event, this meeting here represents the official project closing event. I want to thank all contributors for their outstanding work. Your efforts are highly appreciated, and we should celebrate the internal and external impact of the game. Caspa's capacity building is complete for now, and he is training a new scholar himself. The development of a serious game is a major achievement, and all stakeholder involved will remember it for a long time. Combining our individual strengths, we collaborated as a team and were able to overcome all internal and external obstacles. I am proud being part of this team. Let's further develop serious games to make the world a place worth living in."

Caspa smiled and gently stroked his wife's round belly.

The Campfire Has Burned Down...

THE CAMPFIRE HAS BURNED down, our story is about to end.

Let me thank you from the bottom of my heart for listening and sharing your precious time with me. I truly hope that you enjoyed the combination of a narrative with a modular process and best practices from

The campfire has burned down—has your game dev story just begun?

all over the world. Allow me to repeat the most important takeaway from this book.

Developing serious games is a highly social procedure. Always keep in mind that you work with and for equal individuals who share their lifetime and creativity with you. Understand the core of their behaviour and treat each other with mutual respect. It sounds too simple, but I promise that this will allow you to resolve 80% of the conflicts in the development process.

Perhaps this story triggered a few thoughts in your mind. Please reflect on these inspirations, select the most promising one and make it real. I would love to hear it, so feel free to reach out and exchange.

I encourage you to take games seriously. To use games as a powerful and necessary tool to address the challenges of the 21st century. Let us use the full potential of serious games and make the world a better place. Together, as a beautiful unity of heterogeneity.

Thank You Notes

First of all, I want to say a huge thank you to Rebekka Schoenefuss, who created the gorgeous illustrations of this book, giving it a unique and beautiful touch. Thank you for your flexibility and bringing this story to life!

Thanks a million to the great guest authors, who made the book a unique mix of perspectives, sharing expertise from all over the world. I feel deeply grateful for your outstanding contributions.

Also, thank you so much for proof reading and your advice allowing me to iterate and improve the book, namely: Alina Hase, Bastian Laier, Jake Manion, Tamer Qarrain, Tim Hoffmann, Troy Dunniway, Philippa Neave, Yane Frenski and Yannic Luteijn.

Thank you very much Will Bateman and the team of CRC press for encouraging me to write this book and offering great support while writing. Thank you for your professional and patient guidance.

A big thanks from the development cooperation sector, collaborating on challenging serious games projects all around the globe, sharing knowledge and working together on the important topics of the 21st century in the past years.

Finally, I feel very grateful to have a loving family and friends at home who support me with all my crazy ideas. You empower me to carry on.

Literature

Beck K., Beedle M., Van Bennekum A. et al. (2001). Manifesto for agile software development (https://agilemanifesto.org).

Braddock, K., & Dillard, J. P. (2016). Meta-analytic evidence for the persuasive effect of narratives on beliefs, attitudes, intentions, and behaviors. *Communication Monographs*, 83(4), 446–467.

Chou, Y. (2014). *Actionable Gamification - Beyond Points, Badges, and Leaderboards. Fremont*. Octalysis Media.

Csikszentmihalyi, M. (1990). *Flow: The Psychology of Optimal Experience*. New York: Harper & Row.

Fullerton, T. (2008). *Game Design Workshop: A Playcentric Approach to Creating Innovative Games*. Burlington, MA: CRC Press.

Hodent, C. (2017). *The Gamer's Brain: How Neuroscience and UX Can Impact Video Game Design*. CRC Press.

Huizinga, J. (1956). *Homo Ludens*. Hamburg.

Nakamura, J., & Csikszentmihalyi, M. (2002). The Concept of Flow Optimal Experience and Its Role in Development. In *Handbook of positive psychology*, 89–105. https://doi.org/10.1007/978-94-017-9088-8_16

Miranda, Eduardo. (2021). MoSCoW Rules: A quantitative exposé. (https://www.researchgate.net/publication/356836488_MoSCoW_Rules_A_quantitative_expose_Accepted_for_presentation_at_XP2022).

Park, C. (2022). Drawing attention to your game. IGDC 2022. (https://youtu.be/he2RIfMeNNM?si=gnIxT67SVMEjABXz).

Patton, M.Q. (2011). *Developmental evaluation: Applying complexity concepts to enhance innovation and use*. Guilford Press.

Patton, M.Q. (2023). The niche and purpose of developmental evaluation. YouTube video. https://youtu.be/X9CplOFsHZ8

Raftopoulos, M. (2014). Towards gamification transparency: A conceptual framework for the development of responsible gamified enterprise systems. *Journal of Gaming & Virtual Worlds*, 6(2), 159–178.

Raftopoulos, M. (2020). Has gamification failed, or failed to evolve? Lessons from the frontline in information systems applications, GamiFIN Conference 2020, Levi, Finland, April 1–3, 2020.

Ryan, R. M., & Deci, E. L. (2000). Self-determination theory and the facilitation of intrinsic motivation, social development, and well-being. *American Psychologist*, 55, 68–78.

Salen, K., & Zimmerman, E. (2004). *Rules of Play. Game Design Fundamentals.* Cambridge, MA: The MIT Press.

Schwaber and Sutherland (2020). 3 (https://scrumguides.org/docs/scrumguide/v2020/2020-Scrum-Guide-US.pdf#zoom=100).

Werbach, K., & Hunter, D. (2012). *For The Win - How Game Thinking Can Revolutionize Your Business.* Philadelphia (USA). https://creativecommons.org/licenses/by-sa/4.0/legalcode and also described in summary

Index

Pages in *italics* refer to figures and pages followed by n refer to notes.

S

For Product Safety Concerns and Information please contact our EU representative GPSR@taylorandfrancis.com Taylor & Francis Verlag GmbH, Kaufingerstraße 24, 80331 München, Germany